Divorce

Other Books of Related Interest:

Opposing Viewpoints Series

The Family

Homosexuality

Current Controversies Series

Family Violence

Gay Rights

Marriage and Divorce

At Issue Series

Gay Marriage

Single Parent Families

Divorce

Christina Fisanick, Book Editor

GREENHAVEN PRESS

An imprint of Thomson Gale, a part of The Thomson Corporation

Detroit • New York • San Francisco • New Haven, Conn. • Waterville, Maine • London

Christine Nasso, *Publisher*
Elizabeth Des Chenes, *Managing Editor*

© 2007 Thomson Gale, a part of The Thomson Corporation.

Thomson and Star logo are trademarks and Gale and Greenhaven Press are registered trademarks used herein under license.

For more information, contact:
Greenhaven Press
27500 Drake Rd.
Farmington Hills, MI 48331-3535
Or you can visit our Internet site at http://www.gale.com

LIBRARY OF CONGRESS CATALOGING-IN-PUBLICATION DATA

Divorce / Christina Fisanick, book editor.
    p. cm. -- (Contemporary issues companion)
Includes bibliographical references and index.
ISBN-13: 978-0-7377-2452-3 (lib. : alk. paper)
ISBN-10: 0-7377-2452-8 (lib. : alk. paper)
ISBN-13: 978-0-7377-2453-0 (pbk. : alk. paper)
ISBN-10: 0-7377-2453-6 (pbk. : alk. paper)
1. Divorce. 2. Divorce--Social aspects. 3. Divorce--Psychological aspects. I. Fisanick, Christina.
    HQ814.D583 2007
    306.89--dc22
                                                    2006022971

Printed in the United States of America
10 9 8 7 6 5 4 3 2 1

Contents

Foreword

In the news, on the streets, and in neighborhoods, individuals are confronted with a variety of social problems. Such problems may affect people directly: A young woman may struggle with depression, suspect a friend of having bulimia, or watch a loved one battle cancer. And even the issues that do not directly affect her private life—such as religious cults, domestic violence, or legalized gambling—still impact the larger society in which she lives. Discovering and analyzing the complexities of issues that encompass communal and societal realms as well as the world of personal experience is a valuable educational goal in the modern world.

Effectively addressing social problems requires familiarity with a constantly changing stream of data. Becoming well informed about today's controversies is an intricate process that often involves reading myriad primary and secondary sources, analyzing political debates, weighing various experts' opinions—even listening to firsthand accounts of those directly affected by the issue. For students and general observers, this can be a daunting task because of the sheer volume of information available in books, periodicals, on the evening news, and on the Internet. Researching the consequences of legalized gambling, for example, might entail sifting through congressional testimony on gambling's societal effects, examining private studies on Indian gaming, perusing numerous websites devoted to Internet betting, and reading essays written by lottery winners as well as interviews with recovering compulsive gamblers. Obtaining valuable information can be time-consuming—since it often requires researchers to pore over numerous documents and commentaries before discovering a source relevant to their particular investigation.

Greenhaven's Contemporary Issues Companion series seeks to assist this process of research by providing readers with useful and pertinent information about today's complex issues. Each volume in this anthology series focuses on a topic of current interest, presenting informative and thought-provoking selections written from a wide variety of viewpoints. The readings selected by the editors include such diverse sources as personal accounts and case studies, pertinent factual and statistical articles, and relevant commentaries and over views. This diversity of sources and views, found in every Contemporary Issues Companion, offers readers a broad perspective in one convenient volume.

In addition, each title in the Contemporary Issues Companion series is designed especially for young adults. The selections included in every volume are chosen for their accessibility and are expertly edited in consideration of both the reading and comprehension levels of the audience. The structure of the anthologies also enhances accessibility. An introductory essay places each issue in context and provides helpful facts such as historical background or current statistics and legislation that pertain to the topic. The chapters that follow organize the material and focus on specific aspects of the book's topic. Every essay is introduced by a brief summary of its main points and biographical information about the author. These summaries aid in comprehension and can also serve to direct readers to material of immediate interest and need. Finally, a comprehensive index allows readers to efficiently scan and locate content.

The Contemporary Issues Companion series is an ideal launching point for research on a particular topic. Each anthology in the series is composed of readings taken from an extensive gamut of resources, including periodicals, newspapers, books, government documents, the publications of private and public organizations, and Internet websites. In these volumes, readers will find factual support suitable for use in reports, debates, speeches, and research papers. The anthologies also facilitate further research, featuring a book and periodical bibliography and a list of organizations to contact for additional information.

A perfect resource for both students and the general reader, Greenhaven's Contemporary Issues Companion series is sure to be a valued source of current, readable information on social problems that interest young adults. It is the editors' hope that readers will find the Contemporary Issues Companion series useful as a starting point to formulate their own opinions about and answers to the complex issues of the present day.

Introduction

On New Year's Day 2004, pop singer Britney Spears married her high school friend, Jason Alexander. Less than two days later the marriage was annulled. While this is undoubtedly an unusually brief period of wedlock, quickie marriages and quickie divorces have become commonplace among celebrity couples. Although most ordinary Americans do not marry and divorce so swiftly, the divorce rate remains high, with just over half of all marriages ending in divorce, according to the U.S. Bureau of Statistics. Although the divorce rate has slightly decreased since the 1980s, divorce remains all too common. While many experts have offered multiple explanations for the high divorce rate—including increased societal acceptance of divorce, larger numbers of women entering the workforce, and overall loss of religious beliefs—the divorce rate shows no sign of further decrease.

Given the high rate of marital dissolution, the rate of remarriage is on the rise as well. Along with these new marriages often come children from previous marriages. In fact, these new families, or stepfamilies, now make up more than 50 percent of U.S. families, according to the U.S. Census Bureau. Demographer Jon Larson has found that one out of every three Americans is now a stepparent, a stepchild, a stepsibling, or some other member of a stepfamily. Demographer Joshua R. Goldstein notes that the odds are stacked against these newly created families because the divorce rate is even higher for second, third, and subsequent marriages. While the risks of failure are high for stepfamilies, the rewards of success can be even higher. If the family can stay together beyond the first few years of adjustment, then they can actually be stronger than most intact families.

Marriages that follow divorce are filled with challenges that are difficult to predict and even harder to manage. Remarried couples run the risk of repeating the same destructive behaviors they engaged in during their previous marriages. Also, newly remarried couples often face the financial consequences of their previous marriages along with dealing with difficult ex-spouses. In addition, couples who remarry typically have high hopes for their second marriages, and when these unrealistic expectations go unmet, it can be a serious letdown for both parties. In fact, some researchers claim that remarried spouses sometimes see their new husband or wife as some form of compensation for their ex-partner. The new spouse is expected to be everything that the ex-wife or ex-husband was not. Unfortunately, argues family psychologist E. Mavis Hetherington, "besides setting a person up for disillusionment, since the new mate may have different but as many foibles as the old, the expectation can also produce marital conflict via shoehorning." In other words, by trying to force the new spouse into a preconceived mold (like using a shoehorn to force a foot into an ill-fitting shoe), he or she will likely become angry and frustrated, which can lead to marital strife and eventual dissolution.

Indeed, it is these fantasies, or unrealistic expectations, that often lead to the break up of remarriages, experts say. More troubling, however, is that tensions can be exacerbated by the presence of children from previous marriages. Many researchers agree that the presence of children from previous marriages is the number one reason why remarriages fail. Newly remarried couples with children who expect the near-utopia of the *Brady Bunch* and other blended-families sitcoms are often shocked to learn just how hard it is to make their new families successful for everyone involved. As journalist Jane L. Mickelson writes, "Stereotypes, preconceptions, and dreams of the perfect family . . . can lead directly to disappointment and failure." In those first few years following the remarriage, Mickelson has found that "the family quickly learns that love and respect do not automatically spring into being merely because a living area is shared." When reality hits, it can increase the possibility that the new marriage will end in divorce.

The risks of failure are especially high for remarriages with children because the relationships between family members are not secure. For example, many children of newly formed stepfamilies are often unsure of how to react to their new stepmother or stepfather. Often they wonder what they should call her or him and if this new marriage will interrupt their relationship with their biological mother or father. The situation becomes further complicated when the new couple has a child of their own. Acclaimed pediatrician T. Berry Brazelton states that "the new baby becomes a symbol of the parents' commitment to their new marriage. Meanwhile, the other children may feel as if they were reminders of mistakes and marriages left behind." Without an open dialogue about these evolving relationships, the children's reactions put the new marriage at risk of failure. According to Hetherington, "Children can be the make or break issue for many second marriages."

Despite these challenges, if a stepfamily can work through the struggles, then they can be successful. Psychology researcher Virginia Rutter found that "after five years, stepfamilies are more stable than first-marriage families, because second-marriages are happier than first marriages." Researchers and therapists alike have recommended many ways for stepfamilies to survive these daunting challenges, including accepting that their new families are not perfect. By looking beyond the fantasies, stepfamilies can assess their own unique challenges and meet them head on. Mickelson, who was a child of remarriage and has raised two stepchildren, argues that these new couples need to "acknowledge the ways in which they are different from the unbroken family. . . . Only then can family members take full advantage of their unique ability to establish an exciting new type of kinship."

In addition to discarding the perfect-family fantasy, step-families can excel if they work together towards establishing a functional, if not ideal, family unit. Researchers Jaelline Jaffe, Jeanne Segal, and Sheila Hutman have found that parents can improve the odds of maintaining their new stepfamilies by tending to four key aspects of stepfamily life: (1) agreeing on financial and living arrangements for the new family, (2) resolving feelings and concerns about the previous marriages, (3) anticipating parenting changes and decisions, and (4) maintaining new marriage quality. Although these tasks might seem daunting, the authors contend that focusing on them even before the remarriage occurs will help ensure that the new family gets started on the path to success.

Even if the newly created family is functioning well, there are still social pressures that may invite tension. For example, *Essence* magazine parenting editor Ylonda Gault Caviness says that American society has not done enough to help stepfamilies survive. She states, "Given the inherent difficulties, stepfamilies sorely need communal support, something that most families take for granted. But the fact is, stepfamilies often don't get the same kind of respect or support from society as their more traditional counterparts." In Caviness's view, society does not view stepfamilies as "real" or "serious" families and are often considered the broken remnants of traditional, intact families. Unfortunately, without community support, these families have a harder time succeeding past those first five years of adjustment. With the assistance of clergy, friends, counselors, teachers, and other community members, stepfamilies can have an easier time making the transition.

In an age when the number of stepfamilies has exceeded the number of intact families, it is essential that the dialogue about marriage and divorce continue. *Contemporary Issues Companion: Divorce* helps illuminate some of the most important debates about divorce and its impact on families and society. By presenting essays, reports, and personal narratives, this volume attempts to bring attention to many issues surrounding divorce and its consequences. Some of these issues, such as whether ending an unhappy marriage is better than trying to make it work, whether divorce is irrevocably damaging to children, and whether the family court system is biased, have been a part of the divorce debate for decades and exemplify how significant and contentious an issue divorce remains in modern society.

CHAPTER 1

Divorce and the
Marriage Contract

The Effects of Prenuptial Agreements on Marriage and Divorce

Carlin Flora

Prenuptial agreements are legal contracts that define how property is to be divided should a couple divorce. These agreements are becoming increasingly popular in an age when it is easier than ever to get a divorce. In the following selection, Carlin Flora interviews two lawyers who debate the impact of prenuptial agreements on marriage and divorce. One of the lawyers, Arlene Dubin, believes that prenuptial agreements provide solid blueprints for managing money issues during and after a marriage dissolves. Sam Margulies, on the other hand, argues that prenuptial agreements may simply indicate that couples are not emotionally ready for a marriage commitment. Flora is a staff writer for Psychology Today.

When Veronica, now 52, was at her father's deathbed, he implored her to get a prenuptial agreement to protect her inheritance. She complied with his last wish, but in turn alienated her future husband. "Even though I didn't have a fortune, he perceived it as a lack of trust," she says. Veronica doesn't think the prenup made their subsequent divorce negotiations any easier. "I don't recommend them; it put up a divide in our relationship. It assumes things will go wrong."

But Jason, a 46-year-old financier now dissolving an eight-year marriage, thinks he is being cheated out of hard-earned money, and regrets not having a prenup. "People [today] marry later, and years of labor may come to fruition during a marriage—labor that has nothing to do with the spouse," he says. "And yet, the law says the spouse gets half." He wishes his financial matters had been settled in good faith at the outset. "Prenups are negotiated when people are thinking of each other as human beings. In a divorce, everybody is out for themselves."

Prenups have grown in popularity in the past 20 years—in concert with no-fault divorce laws, which allow divorce without evidence of adultery or abandonment. But the betrothed and their lawyers remain passionately divided on whether prenups prevent heartbreak.

Consider Arlene Dubin, who keeps her prenuptial agreement in a Tiffany bowl, along with her dried wedding bouquet. A family law attorney and partner at Sonnenschein Nath and Rosenthal in New York City, Dubin is on a mission to rehabilitate the prenup. She believes it is not only a vaccine against a contentious divorce but a blueprint for negotiating money issues before they wreak havoc in marriage.

Sam Margulies deems the prenup antithetical to romantic commitment. An attorney and divorce mediator who practices in New Jersey and North Carolina, Margulies argues that current divorce laws mandate a fair and equitable distribution of assets, making the prenup the stuff of power plays—and tangible proof that a couple is not ready to tie the knot. PT [*Psychology Today*] spoke to both lawyers about the portentous document.

Effect on Marriage

PT: Is the prenup harmful to marriages?

Dubin: No. Disclosure of money issues strengthens the emotional bond. And when people are forced to think about the ramifications of divorce up-front, they are more likely to consider their behavior and actions when in the marriage.

Margulies: No, but . . . If you need a prenup, you probably shouldn't get married. The need for the prenup is the symptom that the relationship will founder. The prenup itself is not going to cause the divorce; it's an indicator of future problems. "They" never want a prenup. One person is trying to render himself invulnerable. And how do you have intimacy with no vulnerability?

PT: Does the wealthier party hold the cards?

Dubin: No. It's impossible to go into a marriage and keep everything. For a prenup to be valid, each party must have a lawyer. The lawyer for the less wealthy partner will attempt to level the field. More and more, the prenup is initiated by the less wealthy party or is negotiated to the advantage of the less wealthy. For example, the man agrees that his spouse will be compensated for nonmonetary contributions to the marriage, such as raising the children.

Margulies: Yes. Struggles over money are really power struggles. The prenup is simply going to memorialize the power distribution that exists. You don't need to work it out in a lawyer's office—you need to work it out in a shrink's office. Without a prenup, the stronger party has got to engage in more compromise in the course of the marriage. But with a prenup, he can just say, "Honey, if you don't like it—leave."

PT: What happens when families get involved?

Dubin: In second marriages, it's legitimate to say: "My children are worried about [their inheritance] if we get married and don't have an agreement." When there is a prenup, the children accept the spouse much more readily.

Margulies: I don't think you should get married if you're not going to put your spouse first. That's what girlfriends are for. If you don't want your wife to get at least a third (the common default stipulation), if you're not willing to share and take risks, why are you getting married?

Tainting Relationships

PT: What about the concept of true love?

Dubin: Romantic love is one thing; marriage is another. It is a spiritual and emotional bond, for sure. But it is also an economic partnership. Whether you have a prenuptial agreement or not, once you get married, you've agreed to the laws. If you think your marriage does not have economic consequences, then you're not living in the real world.

Margulies: Romantic love suggests loving with abandon, risking all and a complete sharing of two lives. It does not contemplate holding back, limiting commitment, separating interests and refusing to risk or share. Yet these are precisely the objectives of the prenuptial agreement.

PT: Do prenups break engagements?

Dubin: I've had occasional cases where people working through the prenup decided not to marry—the prenup in those cases didn't prevent marriage, it prevented divorce.

Margulies: I've seen the process of negotiating prenups break up a lot of people—particularly, when two adversarial lawyers are involved. Lawyers are unable to help foster a relationship. They're very good at destroying them.

PT: If a marriage fails, does a prenup make divorce less painful?

Dubin: Yes. If you have financial arrangements set, there's still going to be emotional issues, but they'll be circumscribed. It's better for the kids; they'll be exposed to less conflict.

Margulies: No. People will challenge the prenup, or they'll say, 'Okay, you got me on the prenup. I'm going to sabotage you everywhere else.'

Prenup Particulars

- Average cost is $2,500 to $7,000, barring the complications of a large fortune.

- Like wills, prenups can be endlessly modified.

- Sunset clauses render a prenup null and void after a predetermined number of years.

- The law regards pets as possessions, so custody agreements about pet care are legally binding. Child custody arrangements are not.

- Lifestyle provisions may be included but are not legally binding. A New Mexico couple, for example, stipulated that they have "healthy" sex five times a week, pay cash unless otherwise agreed and turn off the lights at 11:30 p.m.

No-Fault Divorce Policies Should Be Supported

Anne Kass

When a couple files for a no-fault divorce, they are stating to the court that no one is at fault for the demise of their marriage and that there is no way of reconciling their marital differences. No-fault divorces are popular because, unlike fault divorces, they do not require one or the other partner to be held accountable for the failure of the marriage. In the following selection, Anne Kass supports the no-fault policy. She argues that a return to fault-only divorce would cost filers more in legal fees, require more judges, and make the process of divorce more traumatic for children. She thinks that the family court system should make more of an effort to focus on no-fault marital dissolutions because these allow couples to make a more amicable split of resources. Kass is a retired District Judge of Albuquerque, New Mexico, and a longtime advocate for children and families.

In 1933, the New Mexico Legislature became the first state legislature to create no-fault divorce. Since then, all states have followed New Mexico's lead.

In 1991, a bill was introduced to the New Mexico Legislature to return fault to divorce cases. The bill was not passed.

Let me suggest that (a) returning fault to divorce law is not a good plan and (b) a better proposal is to remove fault altogether, which we've not really done so far.

Arguments Against Fault Divorce

Arguments against returning fault to divorce include the following:

First, returning fault to divorce would cause people to incur far greater legal fees than they already do. That is so because proving fault is very time-consuming, and lawyers' time is very expensive. Because the single greatest problem most divorcing families face is too little money, an increase in their legal fees would make their problems worse.

Secondly, putting fault back into divorce would certainly require more judgeships. That is so because many more divorce cases would go to trial, where they now settle out of court. Neither party would agree that he or she was at fault, and fault would have to be proven at trial. Also, the trials would be longer, as each side would bring in friends, neighbors and relatives to testify about the misdeeds of the other spouse. It costs New Mexico taxpayers $200,000 annually for each judgeship. Returning fault to divorce would make the state's money problems worse.

Thirdly, returning fault to divorce would inflict even more trauma and injury on the children of divorcing parents. Children suffer greatly when they hear anyone criticize or denigrate either of their parents. If fault were an issue, the level of disparagement would increase dramatically, which would make the children's problems worse.

The 1991 New Mexico Legislature wisely declined to pass the fault bill.

However, I believe that, while we have no-fault divorce as a matter of law, we do not as a matter of reality.

Virtually every couple I've seen has analyzed the break-up of their relationship on a fault basis. Moreover, until a very few years ago, lawyers were trained to do fault-based analyses exclusively. In my experience, fault is all too alive and well in divorce cases.

Rather than promote the concept of returning fault to divorce, I believe it better to work towards removing fault in fact as well as in law.

Having observed hundreds of divorcing couples, each partner alleging the break-up to have been the other's fault, I am convinced that it is virtually impossible to fix the fault for a damaged relationship on only one party. Both spouses contribute to the failure.

Focus on Fault Is Detrimental

Moreover, the on-going focus on fault analyses has enormously detrimental consequences to the families in addition to the financial expense.

First, it requires the expenditure of vast amounts of time and energy, as well as money, to try to prove fault. This diverts time, energy and money from positive goals, such as enhancing earnings or improving parenting skills. It diverts time, energy and money from planning the future to sorting out the past.

Next, allowing or encouraging a divorcing party to center his/her attention on the other party's fault inhibits introspection, which is necessary if one is to learn from one's past mistakes. Fault analysis is the shifting of responsibility to someone else. This shifting of responsibility is, I think, one of the greatest shortcomings of the American culture, and its unhappy consequences touch every aspect of our society, but it particularly impedes development of sound personal relationships.

Also, as couples attempt to prove fault, they greatly increase their hurt and anger which, of course, has an awful impact on their ability to cooperate in the future. Future cooperation is essential for divorced couples in many ways, the most important being raising their children.

Options for Reform

I have thought that another way for the legal system to address the problems would be as follows:

1. Reorient lawyers from fault analyses. This goal can be advanced by compelling law schools to teach alternative dispute resolution techniques and by teaching conflict resolution at all levels of education.

2. Make equal division of property and debts the rule. Equal is the law in New Mexico, but elsewhere the rule is "equitable" division. The concept of "equitable" is tied to the concept of "fault". There is no question that an equal division is often inequitable, particularly in cases where the parties have unequal earning power or separate property, but that problem can and should be fixed by step 3.

3. Once the property and debts are divided equally, a future cash flow analysis should be done and money shifted around. If there are children, one goal could be to create two homes with comparable material comforts. In any case, future economic survival is the standard, and it should have nothing to do with who did what in the past.

Essentially, we need to develop some no-fault principles to guide the allocation of limited resources, which is what divorce is really all about.

The historical experience of tying divorce remedies to fault clearly demonstrated that fault was an unwholesome factor. Changing from fault to no-fault divorce was, and is, a good idea.

The problems we are now experiencing under no-fault do not stem from the no-fault philosophy, but rather stem from the fact that to date no-fault has not developed beyond the theory phase. Before we consider returning to fault, we should first develop no-fault from mere theory to actual practice.

No-Fault Divorce Policies Cheapen the Marriage Commitment

Dennis E. Powell

Before the 1970s, divorce was more difficult to obtain in the United States than it is now. Couples who wanted to go their separate ways had to determine that one or the other was at fault for their marriage's failure. Finding fault necessarily required proof of the allegation, which could include adultery, alcoholism, and other problems that made the marriage inhospitable for one or the other party. In the late 1960s, following California's lead, a number of states enacted no-fault divorce laws, which allowed a couple to divorce for "irreconcilable differences," which did not require proof or even allegations of fault on the part of either party. Supporters of no-fault divorce argue that it is a necessary and fair way to end a marriage that is not working for a variety of reasons, while those in opposition to the law find that it just makes marriages easier to end. In the following selection, Dennis E. Powell draws on his own recent experiences with no-fault divorce in the state of Connecticut to explain why he thinks no-fault divorce has harmed the institution of marriage. He asserts that marriage is no longer taken seriously and no-fault divorce laws support this attitude. Instead, he strongly believes that family laws should support marriage so that it remains a serious commitment. Powell is a freelance author who writes about a variety of topics from social issues to technology trends.

Dennis E. Powell, "Divorce-on-Demand: Forget about Gay Marriage—What about the State of Regular Marriage?" *National Review*, October 27, 2003. Copyright © 2003 by National Review, Inc., 215 Lexington Avenue, New York, NY 10016. Reproduced by permission.

Much has been made, and rightly so, of the campaign to permit marriages between persons of the same sex. But even if that campaign were to succeed, its proponents would likely find their victory a hollow one. That is because marriage as an institution has been so thoroughly dismantled and devalued that today it carries just about the same moral weight as—and somewhat less legal authority than—a contract for cellular-phone service. In most states, according to the Rocky Mountain Family Council, it's easier to get out of a ten-year marriage than it is to be rid of an employee hired one week ago.

I have recently gained the ability to comment advisedly on the subject, for my marriage is the target of a modern "no fault" divorce. As it has unfolded, I have discovered how my state—Connecticut—has done all it can to make ending a marriage easy, while making little or no provision for preserving it. In Connecticut, as in other states, "no fault" divorce means "divorce because it suits the mood of at least one partner." The state has produced an official publication, the "Do-It-Yourself Divorce Guide," to make getting a divorce as simple as mounting a defense against a speeding ticket—even if your spouse has no interest in divorce.

Especially if your spouse has no interest in divorce. The "Do-It-Yourself Divorce Guide" offers everything one needs to know to obtain a divorce, but no guidance as to how one who opposes a divorce might respond. There is plenty on how to battle for a bigger piece of the marital corpse and on getting court orders of alimony, child support, custody, and exclusive use of the family home. There is no mention of another pre-judgment court order (a *pendente lite*, as such things are called) available under the law, in which the court may order two sessions with a marriage counselor or other person trained in the resolution of disputes within families. This unmentioned provision is the law's sole nod to the preservation of the marriage.

Filing for Divorce

Filing for divorce, the guide notes, is a simple matter. Fill out a couple of forms, take them to the court clerk, and have copies delivered to your spouse by a process server. The divorce complaint, the second of the forms (the first is the summons, common to all lawsuits in family court), requires the grounds for the divorce to be stated as follows:

A divorce is being sought because: (Check all that apply)

This marriage has broken down irretrievably and there is no possibility of getting back together. (No fault divorce)

Other (must be reason(s) listed in Connecticut General Statute s. 46b-40(c))

The copy of the form served on me by State Marshal Frank R. DeLucia has the first of these choices selected. To demonstrate how meaningless the sentence is in practice, a little background is necessary, using my case as an example.

When on the morning of May 7 my wife seemed troubled, I inquired as to why. She was at first reticent, but when I persisted she said, "I want us to be good friends but not married anymore." I was stunned.

My wife—she is still that as of this writing—is an attractive, intelligent, educated woman, a lawyer who graduated with honors from an Ivy League law school. She has no passion for the law, and her chief concern, or at least the one she has chiefly voiced, is that as a writer I do not make enough money to pay the bills and, ultimately, allow her to quit her law-firm job. Ours was (is?) a marriage that by many standards would not seem unduly troubled at all. Sure, there have been the occasional bumps, but they certainly did not result in either physical or verbal abuse, or even much raising of voices. Mostly, it has been warm and—I thought—happy. Still, my wife thought (and thinks) that divorce is the only answer. I disagree.

Connecticut has a remedy for such disputes: As long as either party wants a divorce, for any reason or for no reason at all, then divorce it will be. The law insists on dissolution of marriage whenever divorce is proposed. The governing case, as the "Do-It-Yourself" guide so helpfully points out, is *Eversman v. Eversman* (1985), in which a Connecticut appeals court found that "the fact that the defendant maintains hope for reconciliation will not support a finding that there are prospects for a reconciliation. . . . A difference, to be irreconcilable, need not necessarily be so viewed by both parties." The effect is to transform divorce from the last resort, as it was before Connecticut passed Public Act 73-373 in 1973, into the first choice. Interestingly, commentary published on the new law at its passage suggests that the "no fault" provision was added for those who agree to divorce. *Eversman* made short work of that notion. . . .

The "defendant"—in most cases the party who doesn't want a divorce—is instructed that he or she may file an "appearance." This means only that the defendant will be informed of filings and events in connection with the case. The defendant may file a "cross complaint," the sole purpose of which is to make the other person a defendant, too. Or he may file an "answer," and it is here that the absurdity of "no fault" divorce becomes especially apparent. Given the presence of two parties—a plaintiff who seeks the dissolution of the marriage and a defendant who very likely does not—one would suppose that there might be some means for the defendant to, well, defend himself. There isn't. . . .

A hearing is then scheduled. Among the subjects covered is "whether the grounds have been proven (which they always are!)," says Ct-Divorce.com, a website sponsored by a Greenwich [Conn.] matrimonial lawyer.

A Brief History of Divorce

In 1997, the percentage of first marriages that ended in divorce was 50 percent. The median duration of a marriage was

7.2 years. This according to "DivorceMagazine.com" (yes, there is such a thing, with the slogan "help for generation 'ex'"). It wasn't always so.

In America, divorce used to be difficult to obtain and, usually, impossible without good reason: adultery, abandonment, abuse, alcoholism. In 1880, according to the historian Robert L. Griswold, one marriage in 21—fewer than 5 percent—ended in divorce. Over time, there have been peaks and valleys in the divorce rate, such as the period immediately following World War II, when returning soldiers found things rather different from how they had left them, or were themselves tremendously changed by war. "But beginning in the mid-1960s," writes Griswold, the divorce rate "again began to rise dramatically, fueled by ever-higher marital expectations, a vast expansion of wives moving into the work force, the rebirth of feminism, and the adoption of 'no fault' divorce (that is, divorce granted without the need to establish wrongdoing by either party) in almost every state." Griswold continues, "The last factor, although hailed as a progressive step that would end the fraud, collusion, and acrimony that accompanied the adversarial system of divorce, has had disastrous consequences for women and children."

Maggie Gallagher expanded upon the injustice of "no fault" divorce in her 1996 hook, *The Abolition of Marriage*: "Divorce is usually not the act of a couple, but of an individual. Eighty percent of divorces in this country are unilateral, rather than truly mutual, decisions. The divorce revolution has not, as is usually claimed, produced a straightforward increase in personal freedom. Rather the divorce revolution can be more accurately described as a shift of power, favoring the interests of one party over those of the spouse who is being abandoned and over those of the children whose consent is not sought."

Like so many things that seemed a good idea at the time and that swept the nation with disastrous results, "no fault" divorce popped up first in California, where it was passed into law in 1969 and signed by Gov. Ronald Reagan. A provision that would have required counseling in contested cases and cases involving children did not make it into the law, which introduced the now-familiar phrase "irreconcilable differences" and which made divorce glamorous and trendy.

In our popular culture the marriage vows now might as well be "as long as the money is good, my spouse's health is not a burden, I don't find someone I like better, for so long as it suits my mood." A matrimonial lawyer in New Canaan [Conn.] put it tragically succinctly: "Marriage is an anachronism. It's a tax status. Nothing more."

No Longer Taken Seriously

No, it is something more, or has become something more. It has become another place where one is freed of the consequences of a decision. Honesty would be served if the first part of every wedding service were, "Ladies and gentlemen, what is about to unfold is devoid of any actual meaning, except perhaps as the prelude to some acrimonious financial transactions."

"After all," the New Canaan lawyer continued, "people are doing everything outside of marriage that can be done inside marriage. They are in committed relationships"—where either party can walk away on a whim, which used to distinguish such relationships from marriage—"they are buying homes, having children . . ." And he is right, though it is scarcely something to say with pride. There used to be things unique to marriage, but those that remain are few and technical. . . .

Which brings us to the bitterest irony in "no fault" divorce. In the old days, a spouse seeking a divorce just because he or she felt like having one needed to persuade the other spouse to play along. A husband wanting a divorce, for instance, would persuade his wife to file for divorce under a phony claim of fault (often "extreme cruelty"); a woman seeking a divorce might talk her husband into offering no defense against her charge of "extreme cruelty." This was Griswold's "fraud, collusion, and acrimony", and it was the leading argument in favor of establishing "no fault" divorce. The effect of "no fault" divorce, however, has been to shift those desperate measures to the spouse opposing a divorce, he or she having been stripped of any other means of saving the marriage. (For example, the spouse seeking a divorce has always been able to say, "If you refuse, I will make your life hell." The argument available to the defendant today is limited to pointing out that the divorce can be made very expensive.) The measures that were so effective in persuading a recalcitrant spouse to go along with a divorce are adversarial in nature; they were effective in breaking up marriages but are useless now that the scales weigh in favor of divorce. If a marriage is not "irretrievably broken down" at the beginning of the process, it is likely to be before the smoke clears.

Across the board, in society and in the law, marriage has become a not-very-funny joke. It solemnizes nothing, signifies nothing, carries no weight, and can be left virtually for the asking. Add marriage to the institutions where one's decisions, actions, and commitments are escapable without much consequence.

Laws Should Preserve Marriage

Yet even for those who believe that marriage is a worthless institution, there are some hard facts that suggest that the law should tilt toward the preservation of marriage. For instance, every study on the subject that I can find demonstrates that divorce increases the likelihood of premature death among spouses on both sides of the lawsuit. Among divorced men, the death rate from high blood pressure and heart attack is double that of their married neighbors: from pneumonia, the rate is seven times as high. The suicide rate among divorced men is four times that of married men. A 1988 study of 20,000 women found that married women were far less likely to become ill than their divorced counterparts, and that, statistically, marriage proved "more important to these women's health than age, education, and family income."

Divorce also fuels poverty. Statistics prepared in 1992 show that more than half of the single-parent households headed by women are below the poverty line. Some of these women, of course, were never married—another accomplishment to which modern society can point with pride—but single motherhood is the likely result when half of all marriages end in divorce. On average, divorce leads to a 30 percent reduction in income for women and a 10 percent reduction in income for men.

How to respond to these data? The clear conclusion is that it is in society's interest to declare marriage a good thing and to seek its preservation. But that was known all along; today, the likely reaction would be to call for new and expensive government programs that will seek (and fail) to cure these ills. (Originating, probably, in California!)

Some argue that the "no fault" experiment has failed and that the time has come to return to a more traditional view of marriage. Maggie Gallagher has proposed a waiting period of several years for a divorce. A few states have introduced legislation that seeks to make it more difficult to get a divorce on a whim. Others have proposed mandatory counseling. But there has not exactly been a rushing wave of support for divorce reform.

There are many who raise their voices against the idea of marriage among same-sex partners. I agree with them. Marriage ought to be between a man and a woman. But marriage ought to be a lot of things it once was but no longer is. Keeping marriage heterosexual may be a good idea, but it has meaning if and only if it is part of defending marriage from the multitude of assaults that have left it a withered, beaten shell of its former institutional self.

Until then, the chief question pertaining to gay marriage is, "Why would they bother?"

Covenant Marriage
Contracts Will Not Lower
the Divorce Rate

Bruce A. Robinson

In an effort to lower the ever-rising divorce rate, small groups of Christian religious leaders and laypersons developed the covenant marriage contract, which makes divorce more difficult to obtain. In the following selection, Bruce A. Robinson offers an overview of covenant marriage contracts. These contracts require couples to participate in counseling before marriage and to prove fault if spouses choose to divorce. Robinson also provides information about states that have already passed covenant marriage laws, including Louisiana, Okalahoma, and Arkansas, and looks closely at the current research on Louisiana's covenant marriage contracts. Given the small number of states that have passed these laws and the small number of couples who choose covenant marriage, it is unlikely, according to Robinson, that covenant marriage contracts will affect the national divorce rate. Robinson is a regularly contributor to religioustolerance.org, an extensive Web site maintained by the Ontario Consultants on Religious Tolerance, a Canadian group he founded in 1995 to help create tolerance among the world's religions through education and discussion.

Both marriage and divorce rates have been in a state of flux in North America, particularly over the past few decades. Divorce rates have skyrocketed, at least in part due to no-fault divorce laws which were introduced across the entire U.S. by the early 1980s. Divorce rates would be even higher if it were not for the large number of couples simply living together

Bruce A. Robinson, "Covenant Marriages: Marriage with a Difference—Harder to Get into, Harder to Get Out Of," Religious Tolerance Web site, www.religioustolerance.org, February 16, 2005. Reproduced by permission.

and informally separating without being married. Divorce is itself a cause of more divorce. As increasing percentage of couples end their marriages, society has become more accepting of divorce. This lowers the bar so that even more spouses choose to bail out of their marriage. The social sanctions against divorce of previous generations have almost completely evaporated.

Some feel that opposite-sex marriages are too easy to get into and too easy to terminate. . . . Covenant marriage (CM) has been promoted as an alternative form of marriage that might increase family stability and lower divorce rates. It consists of a return to divorce based on fault, coupled with premarital counseling. CM is available in three states in the U.S. These marriages are more difficult to get into and more difficult to escape from. Before a couple can marry, the legislation typically requires that the couple engage in premarital counseling and sign a covenant marriage contract. Termination of a CM by divorce typically requires either a long period of separation, or proof of the guilt of one spouse—generally some form of abuse or adultery. The legislation may also require the couple to seek counseling before considering a divorce.

Promoters of CM hope that it will motivate couples to take a long, sober look at their relationship before they decide to marry. The end result, promoters hope, will be more stable, happier, long-lasting marriages.

Little Impact on Divorce

It is doubtful that CM will have much impact on the North American divorce rate:

- Louisiana introduced CMs in 1997; Arizona in 1998 and Arkansas in 2001. The movement then seems to have ground to a halt. As of 2005-FEB, no additional states [have] passed enabling legislation. CM is not an option in the remaining 47 states, or in the District of Columbia, or in Canada.

- Only a very small percentage of couples in these three states are choosing CMs:

- 2% in the case of Louisiana in the years immediately following the passage of their law.

- By the end of 2001, "Fewer than 3 percent of couples who marry in Louisiana and Arizona take on the extra restrictions of marriage by covenant."

- The vast majority select "ordinary" marriage with its access to easy, no-fault divorce. . . .

The Roman Catholic Church has had a form of very restrictive CM in place for centuries. It is the only option that they offer. Once married, the couple can obtain a civil divorce. However, the church still regards them as being married. Marriage is intended for life. In certain cases, an annulment can be granted, but only if it can be proved that no legitimate marriage was ever originally entered into. Perhaps the priest's license had expired, or one of the spouses planned to remain childless, or one of the spouses did not fully accept the permanent nature of marriage.

Henri Mazeaud proposed a form of CM to the French Civil Code Reform Commission in France during 1947. It would have added a clause to the marriage code: "A divorce cannot be pronounced unless at the time of the celebration of the marriage the spouses did not declare that they were contracting a marriage that was indissoluble by divorce. This declaration is received by the officer of the state who registers the marriage." He felt that spouses should be free to choose whether they wanted to enter a marriage that would allow a divorce or one that was indissoluble. It would force the couple to openly declare their concept of marriage before they married.

Mazeaud agreed during discussion before the Commission that some divorces could be beneficial to the individuals. But he felt that it was always bad for society. Divorce would be impossible for those who have declared their marriage to be indissoluble. If there were no "exit door offered by divorce, everything would have been worked out." But there always remained the option that the couple could separate and live apart if the relationship were to break down. Mazeaud's proposal was rejected by a vote of 9 to 12.

In 1995, Christopher Wolfe was a professor of political science at Marquette University and president of the American Public Philosophy Institute. He resurrected Mazeaud's concept in an article published in *First Things* during 1995. He noted that the current law, which permits divorce, ". . . does not permit people to really bind themselves to a permanent and exclusive marriage by reinforcing the personal commitment with the force of the law." Given the option, ". . . they might choose not just to 'commit' themselves to their spouses, but to 'bind' themselves to their spouses. Why should they be precluded from adopting such a strategy?" His proposal, which he was uncertain should be implemented, would still allow for marital separation. However, it would not allow remarriage for either party.

The first CM law became effective on 1997-AUG-15 in Louisiana. It was far less stringent than either of the proposals by Mazeaud or Wolfe. It required the couple to sign a statement of intent, recite a declaration and show that they had completed a course in premarital counseling. A divorce would be granted if fault could be proven on the part of one spouse: having committed adultery, being imprisoned for a felony, [having] abandoned the matrimonial home for at least a year, or [having] committed sexual or physical abuse on a family member. Alternatively, the couple [could] obtain a divorce if they had lived apart for a long interval. . . .

About Covenant Marriages

Those who promote covenant marriages hope that they will change society's conception of marriage. Opposite-sex couples in a committed relationship who marry in certain states now have the choice of entering into either of two types of marriages:

- *A contract marriage.* This is the conventional type of marriage—the only one available in 47 of the states and D.C. All the couple typically needs is some money to purchase a marriage license, two witnesses, and the cooperation of a person licensed by the state to perform marriages. If the marriage turns sour, they can get a divorce under their state's no-fault divorce law, claiming marriage breakdown due to irreconcilable differences.

- *A covenant marriage.* They still need money, a license, witnesses and someone licensed to perform marriages. But there are a number of other restrictions. The law in Louisiana is typical:

- They must go through premarital counseling before they can be married.

- They [must] sign a contract which says that they have chosen their *"mate for life wisely."* The contract also commits the couple to seek counseling if their marriage becomes troubled.

- They can only get a divorce if one spouse:

  - Can prove that the other committed adultery,

  - Has been sentenced to be executed or to hard labor,

  - Physically or sexually abused the other spouse or a child, or

  - Abandoned the home for a year.

Alternatively they can obtain a no-fault divorce if they:

- Have been legally separated for a year or more.

- Have lived apart for at least three years and can prove that they have obtained counseling.

The laws that have been passed to date have a number of factors in common:

- Existing marriages are not affected.

- People with "ordinary" marriages can elect to opt-into a covenant marriage.

However, some states have considered alternative approaches to improve the longevity of marriage. These include:

- Abolishing conventional marriages and offering only covenant marriages.

- Abolishing no-fault divorce.

- Requiring all couples to go through approved premarital counseling before obtaining a marriage license.

- Adding courses to the public school curricula to teach students how to communicate more effectively, how to resolve conflicts better, and how to improve interpersonal relationships, family life and intimacy. . . .

Louisiana Covenant Marriage Act of 1997

Louisiana became the first state to offer covenant marriages. The marriage act was changed on 1997-JUL-15 and came into effect on 1997-AUG-15. It requires couples to complete a statement of intent, recite a declaration, and prove that they have gone through premarital counseling. There is a provision in the law so that already-married couples can convert their relationship to a covenant marriage.

Arizona Covenant Marriage Law of 1998

Senate bill 1133 is titled the *"Arizona Covenant Marriage Law of 1998."* It was signed into law by the Governor on 1998-MAY-21, and came into effect on AUG-21. It requires:

- The couple to sign a declaration in which they state that:

- They regard marriage as a lifelong relationship.

- They have chosen each other carefully.

- They have received premarital counseling.

- If they experience marital difficulties, they commit themselves to take all reasonable efforts to preserve their marriage, including counseling.

- They promise to love, honor and care for one another until death.

- The couple prove that they have completed marital counseling.

A divorce for a spouse in a covenant marriage may only be granted upon proof that the other spouse has:

- Committed adultery, or

- Habitually abused drugs or alcohol, or

- Been imprisoned for a felony, or

- Has abandoned the home for at least 12 months before the spouse files for divorce, and refuses to return, or

- Committed physical abuse, sexual abuse, domestic violence, or emotional abuse against their spouse, a child, or a relative living in the home.

An alternative ground for divorce is separation for a period of time (12 or 24 months, depending upon various criteria).

Even if the above grounds are not present, a divorce may be granted if both spouses agree to a dissolution of their marriage.

- A spouse in a covenant marriage can obtain a judgment of judicial separation if they have first obtained counseling and if:

  - The other spouse has committed adultery, has been imprisoned for a felony, has committed domestic violence or physical, emotional, or sexual abuse of the spouse, a child, or a relative who lives in the home, or

  - They have been living apart without reconciliation for 24 months, or

  - The other spouse has rendered their living together insupportable due to habitual intemperance or ill treatment, or

  - The other spouse has habitually abused drugs or alcohol.

The law provides a procedure whereby a couple who are already married may declare theirs to be a covenant marriage. They do not have to provide proof of marital counseling.

Arkansas: Covenant Marriage Act of 2001

The divorce rate in Arkansas is one of the highest in the U.S. Legislators were motivated to create a provision for covenant marriages as an effort to reduce the rate of marriage failure.

House Bill 2039 is titled "Covenant Marriage Act of 2001." It become law in 2001. It provides for:

- Marriage licenses to have a statement of intent to be completed by one or both spouses that they ". . . declare our intent to contract a Covenant Marriage . . ."

- Spouses to sign a declaration of a covenant marriage in which they state that:

- They regard marriage as a lifelong relationship.

- They have received premarital counseling.

- They have read the Covenant marriage Act of 2001.

- If they experience marital difficulties, they commit themselves to take all reasonable efforts to preserve their marriage, including counseling.

- They promise to love, honor, and care for one another until death.

- A divorce for a spouse in a covenant marriage may only be granted upon proof that the other spouse has:

  - Committed adultery, or

  - Been imprisoned for a felony or *other infamous crime,*" or

  - Committed sexual or physical abuse on a spouse or child.

An alternative ground is separation for a period of time (12, 24, or 30 months, depending upon various criteria).

- A spouse in a covenant marriage can obtain a judgment of judicial separation if they have first obtained counseling and if:

  - The other spouse has committed adultery, has been imprisoned for a felony, or has physically or sexually abused the spouse or a child, or

  - They have been living apart without reconciliation for 24 months, or,

- The other spouse has rendered their condition intolerable, for example by habitual drunkenness for one year, or by *"cruel and barbarous treatment."*

Already-married couples may designate their marriage to be a covenant marriage.

One wonders what the definition of an "infamous crime" is. . . .

Covenant Marriage in Louisiana

The Center for Family and Demographic Research at Bowling Green State University in Ohio issued a report in 2002-JUN containing the results of their study of covenant marriage (CM). They compared a group of covenant and "standard married" newlywed couples in Louisiana. The Center studied 538 couples who married in the state during 1999 and 2000—two to three years after Louisiana activated its CM law.

In their review of the literature, they found that some investigators have concerns about CM. Some have suggested that:

- Marital counseling requirements, lengthy waiting intervals, and the expectation that the couple will remain together at all costs places spouses and children in a failing marriage at greater risk for abuse.

- CM may reinstate the worst features of fault-based divorce.

- CM may create a "conflict of laws" problem: one state's CM legislation may or may not be recognized when couples relocate to a different state. If other states acknowledge the U.S. Constitution's full "faith and credit" clause then they would have to enforce a CM even if contracted in another state. This may result in a precedent that could eventually lead to interstate recognition of same-sex marriage—a possibility that most CM supporters are very strongly opposed to.

- The entire rationale behind CM is that a couple cannot easily obtain a divorce. However, a CM spouse can simply go to another state to divorce. This could bypass many of the features of CM in their state of residence, such as long waiting times, the requirement for counseling, etc. More affluent couples could easily exercise this loophole; poorer couples would be penalized.

- If there are two types of marriages, individuals and groups might pursue still other forms of marriages or unions in the future.

- Divorce based on marriage breakdown and separation might take considerable time to complete. This might delay spousal and child support, leaving some spouses and children in poverty.

- CM couples whose marriage has broken down may try to feign adultery or some other fault-based activity in order to get a faster divorce.

- When spouses, their lawyers, and the court concentrate on assigning fault or moral blame for the failure of the marriage, they may be distracted from more important issues, like custody arrangements for children and the division of assets.

- Legislators might concentrate on creating CM legislation and thereby ignore other approaches that might have a greater effect on reducing divorce rates; e.g., offering incentives for premarital counseling, courses in communication, courses in marital skills, etc.

There are major arguments suggested in favor of CM:

- Couples entering a CM will be inclined to take the marriage more seriously, because the procedure is more demanding and involved.

- Couples whose marriages are in difficulty will find that the legislation and their promises will make separation and divorce more difficult. They will probably feel pressured into making greater effort to preserve the marriage.

- CM may lower, not raise, the level of family violence because the abusing spouse will be shamed for his/her actions during counseling.

The Center's study, and others, found that the couples who chose CM had similar childhood and economic histories, age, education, courtship experiences. But the covenant and standard married couples differed in most of the other factors studied.

Covenant married couples, on average, when compared to standard married couples:

- Are younger: wives by two years and husbands by three years.

- Have greater educational attainment.

- Are less likely to have lived together before marriage (27% vs. 64%).

- Have less complicated union and parenthood histories.

- Are much less likely to bring children into the new marriage.

- Are more likely to have received initial support from friends and family when they announced their engagement.

- Are more likely to have engaged in premarital counseling (99% vs. 46%).

- Have developed more effective conflict resolution strategies.

- Are far more religious.

- Consider that religion plays a more important and central role in their life.

- They are less likely to be Roman Catholic (30% vs. 69%). This difference may be due to the Church's initial opposition to CM because the law required counselors to discuss grounds for divorce during premarital counseling.

- They are more likely to be Baptist or other Protestant.

- Find that their spouse is less likely to act with sarcasm or hostility.

- Are far more traditional in beliefs.

- Have stricter beliefs about different roles for men and women.

- Feel a greater social duty to bear children.

- Feel that when they enter a CM they are making a political and moral statement to their culture.

The researchers conclude that the future will show that covenant marriage may be associated with lower divorce rates. However, an increase in success at marriage may be unrelated to the legal requirements of CM. It may be because couples entering a covenant marriage are quite different from those entering a "standard" marriage. They write: "At the moment, covenant marriage appeals to a small, distinct group who differ in important ways from the average person approaching marriage. Based on the evidence we have at the moment, there is little to suggest that covenant marriage will soon appeal to a larger, more diverse population."

Same-Sex Marriages Raise New Divorce Issues

Kathleen Burge

In the following selection, Kathleen Burge discusses the importance of the right of gay couples to divorce. She argues that while the 2003 Massachusetts Supreme Judicial Court decision to allow same-sex marriages was significant, the power to divorce that came along with the right to marry is likely to be much more important for gays in the long run. Up until the Massachusetts ruling, same-sex couples did not have any protection under the law when their relationships ended, which meant that assets built up over the course of the relationships had to be divided by each couple. Often the less fortunate partner ended up even further disadvantaged. Burge is quick to note the many possible legal predicaments involved when a same-sex civil union is dissolved, including whether or not it would be possible for couples to get divorced in states that do no recognize same-sex unions. While the Massachusetts Supreme Judicial Court has already made a number of rulings in regard to other same-sex family issues, it is clear that not all of the issues surrounding same-sex divorce have been resolved. Nonetheless, she contends that the right to divorce is another step in guaranteeing equal rights for homosexual couples. Burge is a staff writer for the Boston Globe.

As the [Massachusetts] Supreme Judicial Court [SJC] decision [of 2003] allowing same-sex marriage was being hailed as a huge victory for gay and lesbian couples, largely lost in the celebration was recognition of an equally powerful benefit that flows from the ruling: the right to divorce.

"People aren't coming out to celebrate the right to divorce," said Suzanne Goldberg, a professor at Rutgers School of Law in Newark. "But it may turn out that the right to divorce is as important to celebrate as the right to marry." . . .

As the SJC became the first state supreme court to rule that same-sex couples have the legal right to wed, euphoric supporters popped champagne corks. Gays and lesbians across the state proposed to their partners, and some began to plan elaborate weddings.

Hardly anyone was thinking about getting divorced. But in a nation where roughly half of married couples split up, analysts expect that a similar number of gay couples who marry would also eventually seek to end their legal unions.

If same-sex couples are permitted to marry, they would be subject to the same Massachusetts divorce laws that oversee the legal breakups of heterosexual couples. "Gay divorce, if this law goes through, will look like anybody else's divorce," said Nancy Van Tine, head of the domestic relations department at the Boston law firm Burns & Levinson.

Divorce Laws as Protection

Lawyers see divorce laws as protection for couples who split up, especially for the spouse who makes less money or wields less power in the relationship. Now same-sex couples who break up, even those who have been together for decades, get little protection from the courts, unless they took the unusual step of signing "a relationship agreement," a formal contract that spells out what will happen in the event of a breakup.

But for most same-sex couples who break up, there is no right to alimony or to a fair division of property acquired during the relationship. Those who take their former partners to court face the difficult task of convincing a judge that they have any rights at all.

"Just showing it was like a marriage isn't good enough," said Elaine M. Epstein, a Boston divorce lawyer. "You really have to show that you have some other cause of action."

For instance, a former partner could try to convince a judge that there was a verbal agreement that he or she would get half the house if they split up, even if the deed is in only one of their names.

Legal Entanglements

Legal analysts have already begun to predict the legal entanglements. For instance, what if a couple marries in Massachusetts and then moves to a state that does not recognize same-sex unions?

"I think all hell is going to break loose when states have to begin to deal with the process of gay divorce," said John Mayoue, an Atlanta lawyer who has written extensively on same-sex unions. "I really think this is where the fight is going to come, and it's going to be chaos."

In Massachusetts, several SJC decisions have already given guidance to judges grappling with issues that involve gay couples and their children. Since 1993, gays have been allowed to adopt their partners' biological children. And [in 2000], the SJC ruled that gays can have visitation rights with their former partner's children.

But less clear, under current law, is whether partners who split up can be forced to pay support to a former partner's child they haven't adopted. [In 2002], Superior Court Judge Spencer M. Kagan became the first in the state to order that a lesbian pay child support to her former partner's biological child, even though she had never adopted the child.

A Case in Point

Jack Venzer says his case demonstrates why same-sex couples who split up need the protection of the courts. During his 20-year relationship, he said, he was the manager of domestic tasks, renovating the 23-room house he and his partner shared in Milton.

Venzer, 49, said he raised their children from previous marriages and planned parties for the law firm where his partner, Joseph Barri, became a senior partner. "A lawyer said to me, 'You're like the stay-at-home housewife of the '50s,'" Venzer said.

But [in 2002], after he and Barri split up, a court threw out his petition for monthly support from his ex, ruling that there was no legal basis for his request. The house where Venzer has continued to live is for sale, and since Venzer's name was on the deed, he and Barri will split the proceeds. But Venzer, who has AIDS, says he has no income and is now unable to work.

"Without the automatic rights that a married couple gets, I'm entitled to absolutely zero," he said.

Barri could not be reached for comment. Epstein, Barri's lawyer, said the two men had resolved their differences. She said the case was not an example of a same-sex couple harmed by the lack of laws protecting their breakup. "It was a very fair settlement, ultimately," she said.

Divorce in Other States

Lawyers say that if same-sex couples are allowed to marry in Massachusetts, it will ultimately be up to the courts to decide whether gay marriages and gay divorces must be recognized in other states.

Couples united in civil unions in Vermont—the first state to endorse legal, marriage-like unions for same-sex couples—have found that only Vermont residents can legally have their civil unions dissolved in that state.

Nearly 6,500 civil unions have been performed in Vermont [since 2000, when] the law went into effect. Only about 1,000 involved Vermonters; of those, 23 have been dissolved.

A Connecticut man tried to legally end his Vermont civil union in a Connecticut court, but the case was thrown out by a judge. In July 2002 the Appellate Court in Connecticut upheld the judge's decision.

CHAPTER 2

Divorce in
Modern Society

Divorce Harms American Social Values

Alex Moore

Divorce rates have gone up in the last century, but critics continue to debate the cause of such increases. While currently 50 percent of all marriages end in divorce, some believe that this rate could drastically be cut if Americans reexamined their views about marriage and divorce. In the selection that follows, Alex Medearis argues that divorce is harmful to American life and values because it promotes and supports selfishness and greed. To decrease the number of couples who choose divorce, he suggests that Americans refrain from marrying young and wait until they are emotionally prepared for such a commitment. Furthermore, Medearis thinks that children are the greatest casualties of America's pro-divorce attitudes. Medearis is a former editor of the Stanford Review.

It's hard to know what is to be made of today's 50% approximate divorce rate. Why is today's rate so much higher than previous generations'? Are we less mature and getting married too young? Do half of our grandparents hate their spouses? Are human beings not meant to have a life partner? All of these questions have been left unanswered. However, as a greater percentage of our society engages in the practice of divorce, the institution of marriage becomes more degraded and the decision to get a divorce becomes more accepted and mainstream. I argue that divorce is harmful to society's values, harmful to children left to single parents and is a propagation of a selfish "get all you can when you can" mentality that disturbingly is gaining steam in America today.

Alex Moore, "The Easy Fix: Has Divorce Become an Acceptable Part of American Society?" *Stanford Review*, vol. 33, no. 3, November 20, 2004. Reproduced by permission.

Americans Are Immature and Selfish

This is a very loaded issue in today's society largely because 50% of people my age can tell you about their own personal experience with divorce. However, my parents have been married for over 25 years, my grandparents for over 70 (Yes, that's ages 92 and 93—married at 22) so I'm giving an "outsider's" look at divorce. I believe that people in today's society are more immature and selfish than our grandparents at the same age. Many people rush to get married in their young twenties without having a strong sense of self. Perhaps today's world is tougher and more competitive professionally than the world that greeted our grandparents. This would mean that people would need more time to grow into themselves and really establish their own personal values system. I believe this is a theory that is possibly true. It's quite difficult to establish yourself in a career today. Schooling and working are both done on intense levels for all people, even those not going to Stanford. Dealing with these pressures could slow down or delay personal development. This could explain the large divorce rate for people who are getting married at young ages; just out of school, etc. I support Dr. Phil's 27 rule to cut out a lot of these divorces. That is, society is unwilling to give you a marriage license until both partners are over age 27. This would force many young couples to live together and learn about each other before being able to jump into marriage.

Children Are Casualties

The main problems in society are created when these young couples have children. What happens to these children? Well, they end up living in single-parent homes for most of their childhoods. The children then have a one-sided childhood where they get larger exposure to one parent. A bidding situation often forms where both parents vie for their children's love, with stuff (usually presents and/or trips), in an attempt to be the favorite parent. This situation is unfortunate because it adds confusion to the new situation. And this is for clean divorces. Ugly divorces can do much worse damage to the child than confusion and a loss of faith in marriage. Many suffer extreme psychological consequences from fighting parents, which themselves are suffering their own problems and therefore unavailable to their children.

All children need the lessons and constant support from a 2-parent unit to have the best chance to develop as confident and productive human beings. The best super-mom or super-dad in the world could never provide the presence required from the other. It's impossible. Some divorced people get re-married and attempt to re-create the family unit with varying degrees of success. I commend these folks that make the best of their situations; however, I don't think this unit will ever be as great as a positive and loving nuclear family that lacks this destructive past.

Anything from great situations to horrible situations are experienced by these children. I argue that one of the most profound side effects of divorce on children is the child's confusion on the foundation of and distrust of marriage. What process in a person's mind has to happen for them to trust marriage for themselves when they are older? Their seemingly perfect parents could not get along. How can they convince themselves their parents were flawed in judgment, were immature or a bad match? Many individuals are able to restore their confidence in marriage, but others will lose their belief in marriage and will imitate their parents by getting divorced from future spouses. This is a shame.

Restore the Negative View of Divorce

What can society do to mend this problem? Beyond Dr. Phil's 27 rule, I think society needs to restore the vision of divorce as a negative occurrence. With divorces so common we have washed out the failure element for those that participate. Divorce is a personal failure. People today often will point to a marriage ending as a "no fault" event. Neither partner is responsible. People change. It happens. I'd like to believe there is something more to it. I think we need to move to restore responsibility to this process. We should force people who want a divorce into mandatory counseling periods before we grant those divorces. That or we should put it on people's permanent records that they have failed in their personal lives. It should reflect on them. We could ask people when they apply for jobs if they have been divorced. We could have the judge who approves divorces put blame and reason on one or both people. Then we should make it legal for employers to ask who and why. This would force people to reflect on their own imperfections. People who get divorced should have to accept some failure. This restoration of the failure element to divorce would send a message to children that they should respect marriage and not treat the institution with flippancy or disrespect. Those with successful marriages would be looked up to more and held up as examples.

To me, rising divorce rates, which I believe are approximately at their maximum, represent a changing American pop culture that undervalues honesty, caring for others and kindness and instead places value on greed, deception and personal gain at all costs. People are more distrustful of their mates than before and see divorce as a solution to their problems. Previously, people would try to work through difficult issues and in many cases those trying times were the foundation for renewed love and improved strength in marriage. Today, people hit hard patches and call it quits. I think we need to evaluate what values we are teaching children. Perhaps we should change our marketing and commercial standards. Perhaps we should stop supporting media that displays marriage as a loose or optional responsibility. A show called *Desperate Housewives* would not be shown to a five-year-old Alex Moore Jr. I don't know what the answer is, but I do know that divorce should be looked down on, as it was in the 1950s. People who get divorces should not be considered evil, but should acknowledge some fault in their personal life. Marriage should be considered an honored, revered and positive institution. Children should have these values reinforced to them by their married parents, television, school and society.

Divorce Is Neither a Modern nor a Particularly American Phenomenon

Alex Liazos

Those who bemoan the impact of divorce on society and the family often portray it as a distinctly modern phenomenon that is best exemplified by America's high divorce rates. In the following selection, Alex Liazos disputes this notion by examining pre- and postindustrial society's rates of and attitudes about divorce. He further explains that many marriages in most other regions of the world end in divorce for the same reasons that Americans' do and at a similar rate. He notes that at one time the divorce rate among the Kanuri in Africa approached 100 percent. He concludes that changing gender roles have largely contributed to the recent increase in divorce rates around the world. Liazos is professor of sociology at Regis College in Weston, Massachusetts, and the author of a number of sociology texts, including People First: An Introduction to Social Problems *and* Sociology: A Liberating Perspective.

When they bemoan what they consider the catastrophe of divorce, writers often say the U.S. divorce rate is a unique event in history. They are mistaken. Divorce was common in gathering-hunting and in horticultural societies, where women were generally equal to men. It became fairly uncommon in patriarchal peasant societies (European, Chinese, and others), where women were socially subordinate to men and unable to leave oppressive marriages. Divorce is now common and increasing in industrial societies outside the United States, including Japan. It is being considered and debated in societies with no or limited divorce, such as Chile and Iran.

Preindustrial Societies

Divorce was easy and simple in gathering-hunting and horti-cultural societies, such as those found in North America. People owned few possessions, so there was little arguing over the division of property when the marriage failed. Men and women contributed equally to the material needs of families, and they lived in small groups where family and community supported all people. Thus, it was little hardship for people to divorce. Moreover, individual freedom and autonomy were basic in those cultures, and people saw no need for anyone to stay in miserable marriages.

When French Jesuits (Christians from a peasant society) came to the Northeast around 1600 to convert Native Americans to Christianity, they repeatedly commented in their annual reports about the ease of divorce [among Indians]. They reported that marriages had no stability, "and are broken more easily than the promises which children make to one another in France." Among the Huron, "the freedom of leaving one another on the slightest pretext is . . . generally admitted as a fundamental law of these peoples"

The Native peoples were puzzled by the Jesuits' opposition to divorce. To them, it made no sense for unhappy couples to stay together. When husbands and wives were unhappy, "they separate from one another in order to seek elsewhere the peace and union which they cannot find together." They saw no reason to spend the rest of their lives together in misery. They could not believe Europeans allowed no divorce. [As one source noted,] "They look upon it as a monstrous thing to be tied to one another without any hopes of being able to untie or break the knot."

Among the Mundurucu of the Amazon in the early 1950s, most people divorced at least once, with divorces occurring mostly in the first two years of marriage. After children arrived, affection grew between spouses and there was no divorce in most marriages. Divorce was a "simple matter." Men left the women's households, where the children continued to live with their other relatives. There was little economic dislocation, since the living compounds of the Mundurucu—consisting of an older woman, her daughters, and their husbands and children—were production groups that supported everyone in the household (so too among the Iroquois and other peoples). In short, children, women, and men did not suffer economically [from divorce].

Thus, divorce has been common in most societies. It even approached [a rate of] 100 percent in some, such as the Kanuri in Africa, where people still married and valued marriage, and where there was social stability.

Reasons for Divorce

Grounds for divorce vary. Among the Mundurucu, "Divorces happen for a variety of reasons. The new husband may turn out to be lazy or inept and sufficiently irritating to his in-laws to be sent off. Or he may experience personal difficulties in the household, leaving him with the alternative of taking his wife away with him or divorcing her; the kin ties of the wife in such cases usually turn out to be stronger than the conjugal bond. The man may leave a woman because she is lazy, or he may discover her in an adulterous relationship and walk out in outrage. Similarly, the wife may become angered with the extramarital affairs of her husband and seek backing from her housemates to divorce him" [write researchers Yolanda and Robert Murphy in *Women of the Forest*].

In summary, [as researchers Emily Schultz and Robert Lavenda put it,] "nagging, quarreling, cruelty, stinginess, or adultery may be cited as causes of divorce. In almost all societies, childlessness is grounds for divorce." ... These explanations are very similar to those Americans give for ending their marriages. To say divorce is common and simple is not to deny the pain, anger, sadness, and disappointment people feel.

Divorce in Modern Industrial Societies

Divorce is common in industrial societies today. It is not uniquely American. Even in Japan, often cited as a contrast of marital stability, divorce doubled from 1968 to 1998, and stood at about the same rate as Germany and France. [Researcher Sharon] Moshavi tells the story of 54-year-old Fusako, who had been unhappy in her marriage for a long time. She searched for a job to support herself and leave her empty marriage, but found nothing and was trapped. Meantime, younger women were attending workshops to learn about their legal rights as they considered divorce. They wanted "more personal happiness and fulfillment from their marriages." But Fusako had "resigned herself to her fate [in a loveless marriage], and she's got advice for any young Japanese woman: If the marriage isn't working, get out fast."

Premarital Cohabitation Increases the Chances of Divorce

Phyllis H. Witcher

In the following selection, Phyllis H. Witcher argues that the ease of obtaining a divorce in the United States has convinced many people not to marry. Instead, they often choose to cohabit, or live together unmarried. Furthermore, Witcher states, cohabitating partners who marry are more likely to later divorce. She believes that the high divorce rate can be lowered if fewer people cohabitated and if divorce and tax laws are changed to support strong marital unions. Witcher is a pro-marriage activist and the founder of Protecting Marriage, Inc., an educational nonprofit organization focusing on family policy issues.

The general public has been told that cohabitation leads to marriage. Some data suggest that cohabitation promotes divorce and often leads to disaster in the family.

Many experts want to believe that cohabitation decreases the likelihood of divorce and offer it as their central reason for supporting the arrangement. Yet by opening the opportunity to unilateral no-fault divorce, people tend to seek more divorces and choose not to marry; they are also more disposed to cohabit. The numbers in support of this situation are alarming.

There are now eight times more cohabiting, unmarried couples than there were in 1970. Since that time, the number of marriages has decreased, to the point that the United States now has its lowest marriage rate in 40 years. When such a vacuum is created, people will move to fill it with an acceptable, if less desirable, replacement.

Phyllis H. Witcher, "Not-So-Cozy Cohabitation," *World & I Online* (WorldandI Journal.com), vol. 19, no. 3, March 2004. Copyright © 2004 News World Communications, Inc. Reproduced by permission.

The reason that marriage has decreased in attractiveness is changes in divorce laws. Specifically, the laws ushered in from 1970 through 1985 have made it quicker and more profitable for an individual to choose divorce and much riskier to receive one. Repeated studies, such as Leora Friedberg's in the *American Economic Review* (June 1998), show that this statutory change to unilateral divorce, independent of all other factors, caused the divorce rate to increase dramatically.

A person's absolute right to many privileges around marriage was expunged from our laws in 1970. When "no-fault" divorce changed the basic procedures, all defenses in court were abolished. That change has had a negative and unpredictable impact, making divorce outcomes onerous. Many people now prefer not to marry in order to avoid the negative consequences of divorce. Let's consider what those are and then examine how to correct the situation.

The Link Between Divorce and Cohabitation

Divorce begets cohabitation. Adults whose own parents divorced are much more likely to choose cohabitation over marriage. This fact has been, perhaps, wrongly interpreted. Some researchers and therapists imply that the propensity to "marital failures" has been passed down to the current generation, as if divorce is a genetic illness or environmental toxin. Fortunately, the influence of a parental divorce on the later cohabitation of their children decreases as the parents' age at divorce increases.

It is not always recognized, but divorce commonly produces a decline in the socioeconomic status of one of the partners, usually the wife. Alimony is rare and, if awarded, rarely paid. Perhaps especially vexing is the fact that children are victimized.

Typically, children of divorce are less well supported than children of intact families. In addition, they do not develop as well psychologically or achieve as much educationally. They are usually less happy and well adjusted than other children, and our schools are overburdened dealing with their problems.

For some, cohabitation may be an effort to avoid the problems caused by divorce. It is now a leading family values issue, as well it should be. The disposition to avoid divorce is often strong among people who witnessed their parents' divorce. Nevertheless, children often suffer more when one member of the cohabiting unit is not the biological parent.

The family form of cohabitation/unmarried families which is counted with step-families in all surveys, is a highly sensitive area that needs examination for policy intervention. In his 2002 report *Marriage: The Safest Place for Women and Children*, Patrick Fagan of the Heritage Foundation observed, "Although the United States has yet to develop the capacity to measure child abuse by family structure, British data on child abuse are available." One such study, by Martin Daly and Margo Wilson, included research from several countries, including the United States. It found that having a stepparent, especially a genetic mother with a boyfriend, is the "most powerful risk factor for severe child maltreatment yet discovered."

Alarmingly, in a cohabiting household where one parent is nonbiological, severe child abuse is 30 times more probable than in households where children are raised by both biological parents. The risk of injury or death is, therefore, similarly increased. Dedicated, credible research on the stresses and challenges within step/cohabiting families is needed if the oft-repeated motto Children First is to become authentic policy.

Ironically, cohabitation between a man and woman decreases the likelihood that they will marry. Moreover, when people who have cohabited decide to marry, they will often later divorce. In "Premarital Cohabitation and Subsequent Marital Stability" researchers Alfred DeMaris and K. Vaninadha

Rao reported that cohabitation prior to marriage is often a predictor of divorce. In addition, promiscuity (cheating outside of a relationship) is actually greater among cohabiting couples. Thus security between cohabiting partners is much less than among married partners.

Many cohabiting couples keep everything economically separate. While this may be a benefit when cohabiting partners are young, the same is not true for the elderly.

Catherine Wannamaker, the author of *Suddenly Alone* (1998), sees frequent media reports of senior citizens, abandoned and homeless, who cohabited in order to retain a deceased spouse's health insurance or preserve eligibility for Medicaid. Some cohabiting partners promise that they have willed a cohabited home to a remaining partner. Promises, however, are no guarantee of receiving willed property. . . .

Decrease Cohabitation and Increase Durable Marriages

The United States has the highest divorce rate in the world; it can be called an abnormal rate. The United Kingdom is ranked second, but its numbers are not even close. An exceedingly modest reduction in the world's highest rate of marital destruction cannot be heralded as a success in policymaking. Stating that the U.S. divorce rate is in a modest downturn ignores the fact that such a reduction is meaningless in human terms. In this country, people must confront the meanest, least conducive environment for marriage and family stability. The widening drift into cohabitation shows that family structures, overall, are deteriorating.

Divorce is a safety valve of significance to any society. Nevertheless, our government cannot pass a law that forces anyone to remain married if he does not choose to do so. The issues surrounding the termination of a marriage (assets, property, children, income protection) cannot be kept unilateral.

The granting of a divorce should not be separated from surrounding issues. Constitutional law provides a responding spouse, man or woman, a right to defend those matters that have been denied under mandatory no-fault divorce. Tellingly, this denial has never been attempted in any other area of our laws. If our divorce laws were altered to be potentially less damaging, cohabiting couples would likely find marriage the better option.

Our legal system needs to stop the trail from cohabitation to marriage to divorce. A shift in power from the cohabitors to the married is recommended by most observers, and it can only be achieved by demanding change in laws at both the state and federal levels. Allen Parkman, an attorney and professor of management at the University of New Mexico, has documented the economic impact of cohabitation and divorce. Parkman emphasizes that federal change in contract law on marriage is needed, as "this preemption of the grounds for [no-fault] divorce by the states has become increasingly questionable."

Changing divorce law (this does not mean outright repeal) is necessary to eliminate the temptation to exploit a woman's desire to marry and have a child and to share that life with the child's other genetic parent. The state cannot interfere, economically, in an intact marriage.

State laws currently require a deserted wife and mother to file for divorce—a divorce she usually does not want—to allow the state to exact financial support for the family from her absent husband. Tax laws need to be changed so that cohabiting couples can no longer escape tax burdens that marriages must accept.

Removing some risks of divorce on demand will decrease the not-so-cozy relationship of cohabitation. By buttressing our marriage laws, we will decrease emotional distress, spousal abuse, and threats to children and elders. Some may have been convinced that "shacking up" had the look and form of marriage, but we know now that it has been a bad bargain. . . .

The desire to love and be loved, to procreate and share that with one's spouse, is life's most compelling emotion. J.R.R. Tolkien, author of *Lord of the Rings*, once spoke of the marriage-related choices that society needs: "Nearly all marriages, even happy ones, are mistaken in the sense that almost certainly (in a more perfect world or even with a little more care in this imperfect one) both partners might be found more suitable mates. But the real soul-mate is the one you are married to."

Premarital Cohabitation Does Not Increase the Chances of Divorce

Catherine L. Harris

In the following selection, Catherine L. Harris argues that studies that point to a correlation between premarital cohabitation and divorce do not fully examine all of the possible variables. She maintains that there may be factors involved in a couple's decision to divorce other than whether they did or did not live together before marriage. Harris asserts that it is important to consider that people who choose to cohabitate before marriage have different values and expectations than those couples who decide not to do so. She argues that these values greatly impact the couples' attitudes towards marriage and must be taken into consideration when discussing any connection to divorce. She concludes, therefore, that there is no proven relationship between premarital cohabitation and divorce. Harris is an associate professor of psychology at Boston University. Her research focuses on cultural psychology and psycholinguistics.

Dueling websites on the internet argue over the meaning of marriage in our lives and whether the current generation of young adults is missing out on a life of fulfillment by pursuing casual relationships into their 20s and 30s. . . .

One piece in this debate are studies, from both the US and Europe, showing that couples who live together before marriage divorce at higher rates than couples who marry immediately. Setting aside the very important question of whether marriage is a route to personal fulfillment, I will explore in this essay reasons to be cautious about inferring causality

Catherine L. Harris, "Cohabitation Before Marriage: Is it a Risk Factor for Divorce?" Department of Psychology, Boston University, http://people.bu.edu. Reproduced by permission of the author.

from studies which show a correlation between cohabitation before marriage and probability of divorce.

Third Variable Problem

For the past six years I've used the cohabitating statistics to illustrate to my developmental psychology class the concept of spurious correlation. This is also called an illusory correlation, or "third-variable problem" because there may be a third variable, other than the variable "did/did not cohabitate", which is the actual causal factor.

I introduce this in class by asking students to come up with non-causal explanations for the statistically valid (and cross-culturally replicable) finding that people who cohabitate divorce at higher rates than people who don't. I present a slide from a *Cosmopolitan* article which blithely assumes causality, in that the writer asks, "Should you live together before you get married?"

Students come up with a wealth of reasons to be skeptical, including:

- The researchers may have been biased, meaning that they chose couples to study who fit their hypothesis. This would mean that the researchers violated the guideline (part of the scientific method) of "systematic observation" when conducting research.

- The difference between the two groups (live together or didn't live together) may be statistically reliable, but like the gender difference in math SAT scores (gender is thought to account for only 3% of the variance in these scores) is such a small effect that one wouldn't want to use it to guide one's own life.

The "third variable" problem is not immediately obvious to everyone in the lecture hall. Some students initially ask if the inferential problem here is that the samples weren't followed long enough, or if what we really need is more information about the two groups.

But with a few minutes thought students readily come up with ideas about "third variables" which get at the following point:

> People who choose to marry without first cohabitating are already a different group of people than those who decide to cohabitate first.

Examples:

- The non-cohabitating group may be more religious. Religious beliefs may be the "third variable" which causes people to forgo pre-marital cohabitation AND causes them to disfavor divorce.

- The non-cohabiting group may have more money, may be more secure in their jobs, or may be older. Being at a secure point in their life may mean that marriage is more attractive, AND financial security may mean there are fewer stresses during the marriage, thus decreasing chance of divorce.

When we draw conclusions from a study, everything has to be the same between the two groups *except* for the variable of interest (in this case, cohabitating or not). Scientists achieve this by randomly assigning members of a population to treatment conditions (marriage or cohabitating). In psychology, we often don't have "experimental control over the variables of interest." The result is that "correlation is not causation" is one of the mantras psychologists learn to repeat.

Looking Closer

So what do researchers do? They try to match two groups on as many of the other potential variables as possible. This would include issues that the callers brought up, such as finances and religious beliefs. But even this won't work, as a thought experiment will make clear.

Scientists often work from experiments of nature. We can imagine an experiment of nature which accidentally ends up effecting random assignment. Imagine a group of couples desiring marriage. After they've decided to marry, a political or natural disaster happens and communities are thrown into relocation camps or disaster shelters. The disaster happens at a time such that some couples have just been married, but other couples' weddings were still pending. In the relocation camps (or shelters) there is considerable privation and confusion, and the couples end up living together regardless of whether they had been able to have a marriage ceremony performed.

What is our prediction? Couples who didn't participate in a marriage ceremony divorce at greater rates? My intuitions don't go this way (or at least not strongly—let me know if yours do.)

You might say, but in this "natural experiment" everyone *wanted* to be married. They were going to be married and then were kept from it artificially. That is why both groups look the same, and why we don't see an effect of which group happened, by chance, to be married before being thrust together in a common living space.

Ah. Exactly. So the important variable is *desire to be married* or *valuing the state of being married* NOT cohabiting before marriage.

Would *Cosmo* have grabbed any attention in their article had the headline read, "Couples who value marriage are less likely to get divorced than couples who don't value marriage"?

We would like there to be easy answers to why marriages work, like, "don't live together." One piece of this seems to be "value marriage." The cohabitation studies may well be making this point. The pro-marriage theorists could mention these studies in terms of whether the desire to cohabitate may be a *marker* of discomfort with marriage. But we should refrain from drawing simplistic conclusions about living together before marriage. There is currently no reason to believe that living together in and of itself—independently of one's values—is a risk factor for later divorce.

An Unhappy Marriage Can Be Worse than Divorce

E. Mavis Hetherington

In the following selection, E. Mavis Hetherington discusses some of the findings of her thirty-year study of divorced families. By following fourteen hundred divorced families, including twenty-five hundred kids, she and her team of researchers concluded that while divorce can be devastating, most adults and children recover from its effects and go on to enjoy productive lives. She urges policy makers to look more closely at studies that show that adults and children in marriages seem to be better off psychologically and physically than those people from single-parent or divorced households. She points out that not all marriages are the same; some are more volatile than others. While divorce experiences are just as varied, most people begin to recover from the effects of divorce by the end of the second year. Hetherington also found that 75 to 80 percent of children and adolescents from divorced families were eventually able to develop fulfilling lives. Hetherington is professor emerita of psychology at the University of Virginia and the author of several books on the psychology of families, including For Better or for Worse: Divorce Reconsidered.

On average, recent studies show, parents and children in married families are happier, healthier, wealthier, and better adjusted than those in single-parent households. But these averages conceal wide variations. Before betting the farm on marriage with a host of new government programs aimed at promoting traditional two-parent families and discouraging divorce, policy makers should take another look at the research. It reveals that there are many kinds of marriage and not all are salutary. Nor are all divorces and single-parent experiences associated with lasting distress. It is not the inevitability of positive or negative responses to marriage or divorce that is striking, but the diversity of them.

Men do seem to benefit simply from the state of being married. Married men enjoy better health and longevity and fewer psychological and behavioral problems than single men. But women, studies repeatedly have found, are more sensitive to the emotional quality of the marriage. They benefit from being in a well-functioning marriage, but in troubled marriages they are likely to experience depression, immune-system breakdowns, and other health-related problems.

We saw the same thing in the project I directed at the Hetherington Laboratory at the University of Virginia, which followed 1,400 divorced families, including 2,500 kids—some for as long as 30 years—interviewing them, testing them, and observing them at home, at school, and in the community. This was the most comprehensive study of divorce and remarriage ever undertaken; for policy makers, the complexity of the findings is perhaps its most important revelation.

Good Marriages, Bad Marriages

By statistical analysis, we identified five broad types of marriage—ranging from "pursuer-distancer" marriages (which we found were the most likely to end in divorce), to disengaged marriages, to operatic marriages, to "cohesive-individuated" marriages, and, finally, to traditional marriages (which had the least risk of instability).

To describe them briefly:

- Pursuer-distancer marriages are those mismatches in which one spouse, usually the wife, wants to confront and discuss problems and feelings and the other, usually the husband, wants to avoid confrontations and either denies problems or withdraws.

- Disengaged marriages are ones where couples share few interests, activities, or friends. Conflict is low, but so is affection and sexual satisfaction.

- Operatic marriages involve couples who like to function at a level of extreme emotional arousal. They are intensely attracted, attached, and volatile, given both to frequent fighting and to passionate lovemaking.

- Cohesive-individuated marriages are the yuppie and feminist ideal, characterized by equity, respect, warmth, and mutual support, but also by both partners retaining the autonomy to pursue their own goals and to have their own friends.

- Traditional marriages are those in which the husband is the main income producer and the wife's role is one of nurturance, support, and home and child care. These marriages work well as long as both partners continue to share a traditional view of gender roles.

We found that not just the risk of divorce but also the extent of women's psychological and health troubles varies according to marriage type—with wives in pursuer-distancer and disengaged marriages experiencing the most problems, those in operatic marriages significantly having fewer, and those in cohesive-individuated and traditional marriages the fewest. Like so many other studies, we found that men's responses are less nuanced; the only differentiation among them was that men in pursuer-distancer marriages have more problems than those in the other four types.

The issue is not simply the amount of disagreement in the marriage; disagreements, after all, are endemic in close personal relations. It is how people disagree and solve problems—how they interact—that turns out to be closely associated with both the duration of their marriages and the well-being of wives and, to a lesser extent, husbands. Contempt, hostile criticism, belligerence, denial, and withdrawal erode a marriage. Affection, respect, trust, support, and making the partner feel valued and worthwhile strengthen the relationship.

Good Divorces, Bad Divorces

Divorce experiences also are varied. Initially, especially in marriages involving children, divorce is miserable for most couples. In the early years, ex-spouses typically must cope with lingering attachments; with resentment and anger, self-doubts, guilt, depression, and loneliness; with the stress of separation from children or of raising them alone; and with the loss of social networks and, for women, of economic security. Nonetheless, we found that a gradual recovery usually begins by the end of the second year. And by six years after divorce, 80 percent of both men and women have moved on to build reasonably or exceptionally fulfilling lives.

Indeed, about 20 percent of the women we observed eventually emerged from divorce enhanced and exhibiting competencies they never would have developed in an unhappy or constraining marriage. They had gone back to school or work to ensure the economic stability of their families, they had built new social networks, and they had become involved and effective parents and socially responsible citizens. Often they had happy second marriages. Divorce had offered them an opportunity to build new and more satisfying relationships and the freedom they needed for personal growth. This was especially true for women moving from a pursuer-distancer or disengaged marriage, or from one in which a contemptuous or belligerent husband undermined their self-esteem and child-rearing practices. Divorced men, we found, are less likely to undergo such remarkable personal growth; still, the vast majority of the men in our study did construct reasonably happy new lives for themselves.

Moving On

As those pressing for government programs to promote marriage will no doubt note, we found that the single most important predictor of a divorced parent's subsequent adjustment is whether he or she has formed a new and mutually supportive intimate relationship. But what should also be noticed is that successful repartnering takes many forms. We found that about 75 percent of men and 60 percent of women eventually remarry, but an increasing number of adults are opting to cohabit instead—or to remain single and meet their need for intimacy with a dating arrangement, a friendship, or a network of friends or family.

There is general agreement among researchers that parents' repartnering does not do as much for their children. Both young children and adolescents in divorced and remarried families have been found to have, on average, more social, emotional, academic, and behavioral problems than kids in two-parent, non-divorced families. My own research, and that of many other investigators, finds twice as many serious psychological disorders and behavioral problems—such as teenage pregnancy, dropping out of school, substance abuse, unemployment, and marital breakups—among the offspring of divorced parents as among the children of nondivorced families. This is a closer association than between smoking and cancer.

However, the troubled youngsters remain a relatively small proportion of the total. In our study, we found that after a period of initial disruption 75 percent to 80 percent of children and adolescents from divorced families are able to cope with the divorce and their new life situation and develop into reasonably or exceptionally well-adjusted individuals. In fact, as we saw with women, some girls eventually emerge from their parents' divorces remarkably competent and responsible. They also learn from the divorce experience how to handle later stresses in their lives.

Without ignoring the serious pain and distress experienced by many divorced parents and children, it is important to underscore that substantial research findings confirm the ability of the vast majority to move on successfully.

It is also important to recognize that many of the adjustment problems in parents and children and much of the inept parenting and destructive family relations that policy makers attribute to divorce actually are present before divorce. Being in a dysfunctional family has taken its toll before the breakup occurs.

Divorce Is Complex

Predicting the aftermath of divorce is complex, and the truth is obscured if one looks only at averages. Differences in experience or personality account for more variation than the averages would suggest. A number of studies have found, for instance, that adults and children who perceived their predivorce life as happy and satisfying tend to be more upset by a marital breakup than those who viewed the marriage as contentious, threatening, or unfulfilling. Other studies show that adults and children who are mature, stable, self-regulated, and adaptable are more likely able to cope with the challenges of divorce. Those who are neurotic, antisocial, and impulsive—and who lack a sense of their own efficacy—are likely to have these characteristics exacerbated by the breakup. In other words, the psychologically poor get poorer after a divorce while the rich often get richer.

The diversity of American marriages makes it unlikely that any one-size-fits-all policy to promote marriage and prevent divorce will be beneficial. Policy makers are now talking about offering people very brief, untested education and counseling programs, but such approaches rarely have long-lasting effects. And they are generally least successful with the very groups that policy makers are most eager to marry off—single mothers and the poor.

In their recent definitive review of the research on family interventions, Phil Cowan, Douglas Powell, and Carolyn Pape Cowan find that the most effective approaches are the most comprehensive ones—those that deal with both parents and children, with family dynamics, and with a family's needs for jobs, education, day care, and health care. Beyond that, which interventions work best seems to vary, depending on people's stage of life, their ethnic group or the kind of family they are in, and the specific challenges before them.

Strengthening and promoting positive family relationships and improving the many settings in which children develop is a laudable goal. However, policies that constrain or encourage people to remain in destructive marriages—or that push uncommitted couples to marry—are likely to do more harm than good. The same is true of marriage incentives and rewards designed to create traditional families with the husband as the economic provider and the wife as homemaker. If our social policies do not recognize the diversity and varied needs of American families, we easily could end up undermining them.

Divorce Does Not Make Adults Happier than Staying in an Unhappy Marriage

Linda J. Waite et al.

In the following selection, a group of researchers funded by the Institute for American Values (IAV) and led by Linda J. Waite found that there is little difference in the quality of life of unhappy spouses who divorce and unhappy spouses who stay married. Using the National Survey of Families and Households (NSFH) administered by the University of Wisconsin, Waite and her colleagues found that couples who rated their marriages unhappy on the 1988 survey were not any happier after they divorced or remarried within the following five-year time period. They compared data from the surveys that rated happiness, depression, self-esteem, and personal success. Ultimately, they conclude that divorce does not make unhappily married people happy. In fact, most spouses who rated their marriages unhappy in the 1988 study rated their marriage happy five years later. Waite is a professor of sociology and the social sciences at the University of Chicago and codirector of the Center on Parents, Children, and Work, at the Alfred P. Sloan Working Families Center. The Institute for American Values is a private organization that works toward strengthening families worldwide by sponsoring studies and publications that seek to better understand the role of families in society and culture.

Does divorce typically make adults happier than staying in an unhappy marriage? Many Americans assume so. This study represents, to the best of our knowledge, the first serious effort to investigate this assumption empirically.

Linda J. Waite, et al., "Does Divorce Make People Happy? Findings from a Study of Unhappy Marriages," Institute for American Values, New York, www.americanvalues .org, 2002. Reproduced by permission.

Using the National Survey of Families and Households (a nationally representative survey), we looked at all spouses (645 spouses out of 5,232 married adults) who in the late '80s rated their marriages as unhappy. Five years later these same adults were reinterviewed, so we were able to follow unhappy spouses as their lives took different paths: in the interim, some had divorced or separated and some stayed married. Because marital strife takes a toll on psychological well-being, the conventional wisdom would argue that unhappily married adults who divorced would be better off: happier, less depressed, with greater self-esteem and a stronger sense of personal mastery, compared to those staying married.

Divorce Does Not Lead to Happiness

Was this true? Did unhappy spouses who divorced reap significant psychological and emotional benefits? Surprisingly, in this study, the answer was no. Among our findings:

- Unhappily married adults who divorced or separated were no happier, on average, than unhappily married adults who stayed married. Even unhappy spouses who had divorced and remarried were no happier, on average, than unhappy spouses who stayed married. This was true even after controlling for race, age, gender, and income.

- Divorce did not reduce symptoms of depression for unhappily married adults, or raise their self-esteem, or increase their sense of mastery, on average, compared to unhappy spouses who stayed married. This was true even after controlling for race, age, gender, and income.

- The vast majority of divorces (74 percent) happened to adults who had been happily married five years previously. In this group, divorce was associated with dramatic declines in happiness and psychological well-being compared to those who stayed married.

- Unhappy marriages were less common than unhappy spouses. Three out of four unhappily married adults were married to someone who was happy with the marriage.

- Staying married did not typically trap unhappy spouses in violent relationships. Eighty-six percent of unhappily married adults reported no violence in their relationship (including 77 percent of unhappy spouses who later divorced or separated). Ninety-three percent of unhappy spouses who avoided divorce reported no violence in their marriage five years later.

- Two out of three unhappily married adults who avoided divorce or separation ended up happily married five years later. Just one out of five of unhappy spouses who divorced or separated had happily remarried in the same time period.

Unhappy Spouses

Does this mean that most unhappy spouses who divorced would have ended up happily married if they had stuck with their marriages? We cannot say for sure. Unhappy spouses who divorced were younger, more likely to be employed and to have children in the home. They also had lower average household incomes than unhappy spouses who stayed married. But these differences were typically not large. In most respects, unhappy spouses who divorced and unhappy spouses who stayed married looked more similar than different (before the divorce) in terms of their psychological adjustment and family background.

One might assume, for example, that unhappy spouses who divorce and those who stay married are fundamentally two different groups; i.e., that the marriages that ended in divorce were much worse than those that survived. There is some evidence for this point of view. Unhappy spouses who divorced reported more conflict and were about twice as likely to report violence in their marriage than unhappy spouses who stayed married. However, marital violence occurred in only a minority of unhappy marriages: Twenty-one percent of unhappily married adults who divorced reported husband-to-wife violence compared to nine percent of unhappy spouses who stayed married.

On the other hand, if only the worst marriages end in divorce, one would expect greater psychological benefits from divorce. Instead, looking only at changes in emotional and psychological well-being, we found that unhappily married adults who divorced were no more likely to report emotional and psychological improvements than those who stayed married. In addition, the most unhappy marriages reported the most dramatic turnarounds. Among those who rated their marriages as very unhappy, almost eight out of ten who avoided divorce were happily married five years later.

Unhappy Marriages That Survive

Other research (and the experience of clinicians) suggests that the kinds of marital troubles that lead to divorce cannot be sharply distinguished from the marital troubles that spouses overcome. Many marriages of middling quality end in divorce. Many marriages that experience serious problems survive and eventually prosper.

More research is needed to establish under what circumstance divorce improves and under what circumstances it is associated with deterioration in adult well-being. Additional information on what kind of unhappy marriages are most (and/or least) likely to improve if divorce is avoided is also needed.

To investigate the latter, we conducted focus group interviews with 55 marriage survivors—formerly unhappy husbands and wives who had turned their marriages around. Among our findings:

- Many currently happily married spouses have had extended periods of marital unhappiness, often for quite serious reasons, including alcoholism, infidelity, verbal abuse, emotional neglect, depression, illness, and work reversals. Why did these marriages survive where other marriages did not? The marital endurance ethic appears to play a big role. Many spouses said that their marriages got happier, not because they and their partner resolved problems but because they stubbornly outlasted them. With time, they told us, many sources of conflict and distress eased. Spouses in this group also generally had a low opinion of the benefits of divorce, as well as friends and family members who supported the importance of staying married.

- Spouses who turned their marriages around seldom reported that counseling played a key role. When husbands behaved badly, value-neutral counseling was not reported by any spouse to be helpful. Instead wives in these marriages appeared to seek outside help from others to pressure the husband to change his behavior. Men displayed a strong preference for religious counselors over secular counselors, in part because they believed these counselors would not encourage divorce.

While these averages likely conceal important individual variations that require more research, in a careful analysis of nationally representative data with extensive measures of psychological well-being, we could find no evidence that divorce or separation typically made adults happier than staying in an unhappy marriage. Two out of three unhappily married adults who avoided divorce reported being happily married five years later.

CHAPTER 3

Divorce and the Family

The Family Court System Is Biased Against Fathers

Rachel Alexander

In the following selection, Rachel Alexander argues that the family court system is biased against fathers when it comes to awarding custody and child support. She takes issue with using the "best interests of the child" as a means for determining who should be given custody. Focusing on two factors of this doctrine, the capability of the parents and claims of domestic violence, Alexander questions its usefulness in custody disputes. She asserts that the parent who is best able to take care of the child should be the parent who earns the most money—and that parent may often be the father. She also argues that mothers exaggerate or fabricate claims of domestic violence against their partners in order to win the court's sympathy. In addition, Alexander posits that child support payments awarded to custodial mothers are often much too high for what is needed to meet the needs of the children, and mothers often do not spend the money wisely. To end these discriminatory practices, she suggests that in situations where both parents want custody of the child, child support should be eliminated and custody should be given to the parent who is more financially capable of raising the child. Rachel Alexander is the coeditor of IntellectualConservative.com, a conservative opinion Web site, and an attorney and policy advisor in Phoenix, Arizona.

Child custody has emerged as an area where men run into a glass ceiling. "It's awful to take a child away from its mother!" Sound familiar? That is because it is the message that has been repeatedly hammered at society by feminists, as well as from some conservatives. But you won't hear the

Rachel Alexander, "Child Custody: Where Men Hit the Glass Ceiling," Intellectual Conservative Web site, www.intellectualconservative.com, 2006. Reproduced by permission.

equivalent, "It's awful to take a child away from its father," because the feminists aren't pushing equivalent respect for fathers. Instead, you are more likely to hear this mantra about fathers, "there's so many deadbeat dads." The feminists have successfully changed the law, the courts, and societal attitudes when it comes to the custody and care of children from split homes. Instead of looking at fathers' capabilities and indiscretions individually, the law makes sweeping assumptions and treats all fathers as second class. Women, if you are successful in no other area of life, read this article closely, because you can easily succeed here, the system is so weighted in your favor. Free money, free legal help, and kind court staff. If you don't work, or don't work much, you'll make out even better, so it is best not to work much. And all you need to do is get pregnant! Men, all I offer for advice to you is this: if you have children, you'd better pray that you remain a couple.

An Unbalanced System

Sad as it sounds, this is where the law is at. When a couple that has mutual children splits up, the courts examine just a few factors to determine custody, known as the "best interests of the child." These factors make it very likely that the woman will get custody of the children and hence child support money. Two of the most important factors include who is better able to "take care" of the child and whether there has been domestic violence by one of the parents. Well, these factors "sound" good, but in reality, they have been specifically selected for their heavy bias against fathers. There are numerous other factors that address equally as serious issues, that could affect mothers for the worse, or at least equally affect both parents, such as drug abuse, but these factors are conveniently not found in the "best interests of the child" statutes (there must be an actual drug conviction—which is absurd—one drug-addict mother was able to take custody away from the father even though she snorted meth every single day—the courts had no knowledge of her drug habit!). "Take care" of the child has little to do with being able to financially support the child. It should, since almost as many women as men work outside of the home now, but because a lot of women with children who split up with the fathers aren't very ambitious and sit around the house watching soap operas, the law has been crafted to label this as "taking care" of the children, instead of earning money. Since most fathers work full-time, they lose here.

"Domestic violence" is another disguised way of guaranteeing that the fathers lose. Women are now trained by society to call the police anytime their boyfriend or husband loses his temper, and are using and abusing this taxpayer funded "helpline" at an increasingly alarming rate. Murray A. Straus, a sociologist and co-director for the Family Research Laboratory at the University of New Hampshire, reported that at least 30 studies of domestic violence, including some he had conducted, found that women were as equally culpable of domestic violence as men. Yet this information is not widely publicized, and is downplayed by both police officers and the courts. Women are also abusing restraining orders. A recent article in *Human Events* cited a government study that found that fewer than half of all restraining orders contained even an allegation of physical violence. Instead of working out their fights, or leaving the man, women are taking the easy way out and forcing taxpayers to pay for their "tattling" every time they take up the time of a police officer or court. Of course, many times it is the woman who caused the fight, but that is not going to end up in the court's minute entry. Men are laughed at if they are the victims of domestic violence. One young father attempted to seek free legal help from a domestic violence law clinic after his ex-wife continued to hit him, and the clinic turned him away in amusement. Another young father had the domestic violence of an ex-girlfriend, who had hit him, used against him in order to justify taking away his child.

It is easy for mothers to obtain free legal aid in pursuing custody of their children. There are flyers everywhere—in women's restrooms, in doctors' offices, and in government buildings, offering free legal resources for women to use. The Legal Aid clinics help out so many mothers with custody disputes and divorces that recently they have had to limit their representation of custody cases to cases alleging abuse. Domestic violence legal clinics are at many of the law schools now, and give women free legal help with divorces, custody disputes, and restraining orders. If there are low-income requirements, they are rarely verified; any woman can come in and say she makes very little money, and on her word alone she will receive free legal help (just like at Planned Parenthood).

Child Support

The child support laws are crafted not just to provide for the cost of raising a child, but to bring the parent receiving the support to the level she would have been at if she were still with the father! The absurdity of this situation can be seen in this all too common example: A woman cheats on her husband and then files for no-fault divorce. She gets custody of their children, AND the benefit of his salary and payraises until their child turns 18 (25 in Massachusetts)—all the money benefits as if they were still married (and she may even get alimony on top of that, but that is a different issue for another column, and at least with alimony, once the mother remarries, the alimony goes away)! Why should an ex-wife be guaranteed, years after having been married, the same living standard of her husband? Absent unhealthy circumstances, why shouldn't the parent with the BETTER living standards be considered the one better prepared to take care of the child? That way, one parent isn't stuck paying for the ex-spouse too. Currently, though, most child custody laws do not consider financial responsibility of the parent as one of the "best interests of the child."

Child support is widely touted by governmental agencies as one of the most important things government does, and the duty of it is glorified almost nazilike to the level of a moral authority. Yet what exactly does child support do? The charts for child support award way too much money to the custodial parent—does anyone really believe that it costs $800/month to raise a child? In most situations, the mother has custody and makes considerably less money than the father. According to fairly standard child support guidelines, if the mother makes $20,000/yr and the father makes $40,000/yr, and there is one child, the father should pay $535/month in child support (the formula adds both parents' salaries together, then comes up with a random number of how much they think that child costs—here it was $800—then has the non-custodial parent pay the percentage his salary is—here it is 66%). Does anyone REALLY THINK that many of the mothers who resort to going to court to collect child support are the types of mothers who would spend a full $535/month on one child, as well as another $265/month of their own money (particularly if the child is older than 5 and in school)? There is no monitoring of that money, and it is very difficult to get a court to order any type of accounting by the mother. One such mother of a 6-year old has stated that she is saving the money for breast implants.

Discouraging Personal Responsibility

Furthermore, the concept of child support money discourages personal responsibility and ambition. It penalizes the custodial parent for working harder and trying to get ahead, because a higher paying job would reduce the amount of free money they receive from the other parent. It is akin to welfare—if you work hard, you aren't eligible for it. And it is a double penalty, because it also penalizes the non-custodial parent for working harder. The more money the non-custodial parent makes, the more money is taken out of his paycheck to go to the residential parent.

Do we really want to heap benefits on mothers who split up with the fathers, essentially giving "reward" money to women who have sex, instead of letting them suffer the consequences? Everyone knows that sex without true commitment leads to broken down homes and emotional trauma, particularly for any children involved. Everyone also knows that when you have sex, you may get pregnant. In some ways, child support is merely a disguised form of prostitution—women are encouraged to have sex and receive money from any man who succeeds in impregnating them. After sex, the man then has no other contact with the woman except to give her money for the child, and any modicum of visitation he can squeak out. Instead of teaching women to avoid gratuitous sex, our society encourages sex with its condom education and giveaways, and easy access to taxpayer-funded Planned Parenthoods. Women realize they can have gratuitous sex without suffering any consequences, because the safety net of a man's pocketbook will always be there for them, thanks to the long arm of the moral authoritarian government child support agency that reassures them that they are right.

And what exactly are deadbeat dads? Many "deadbeat dads" are simply fathers who are going through a hard time economically; they may have lost a job, or simply are having a difficult time paying $800/month in child support. Sure there are some fathers who have completely rejected any responsibility towards their children, but that doesn't mean all fathers should be treated like criminals and rounded up by Sheriff's Offices and taken into jail. Why are the fathers held accountable while the mothers aren't?. . .

Practical Solutions and the Child's Best Interests

So what should the solution be? For starters, how about ending child support between parents who both want custody of their children? If someone really wants their children, they will find a way to make ends meet. It just doesn't cost that much to raise a child, no matter what people whine. The message we should be sending is, if you can't afford a child, then abstain from sex! Foster parents receive around $300/month per child. This isn't very much money. Nobody seems to complain about those children not receiving $800/month. Why not let the parent who wants to care for the child, and is more financially capable, have the custody, or at the very least cut out the child support? That way, no parent is stuck supporting the other parent. This would also send a message to parents that they should be ambitious and set good work ethics for their children, instead of the current message which encourages parents to be lazy and earn less. If the mother has to work during the day, and the father works evenings, let the father take care of the children during the day instead of putting them in daycare. There are better workable solutions than giving the children to the mother just because she is lazy and stays at home, utilizing the father only as a money funnel. One mother sat around the house getting high on her days off, yet still put her child in daycare, using the father's money!

Finally, "domestic violence," which has been abused by women, should be looked at more closely by the courts if it is to be a factor in determining child custody. There may be more to "domestic violence" than appears in a brief minute entry or police report. For example, the mother may have been racked out on drugs at the time she called the police, as well as every day of her life, yet this is not taken into consideration as part of the "best interests of the child" unless there is an actual drug conviction. The courts should also examine whether the mother is the type to move from abuser to abuser, which ultimately creates an unstable upbringing for the child. Is it really better that a child stay with a mother who cycles through violent or volatile relationships, or is it better that the child live with the father whose only "history of domestic violence" occurred when the mother obtained dubious restraining orders against him when she was having affairs on him? Unfortunately, the laws do not currently take these circumstances into consideration when considering the "best interests of the child." Unless a father has an excellent attorney who is able to get ahold of hard evidence proving these types of circumstances, and has success persuading a judge to give these factors some weight even though they are not in the law, a father is simply out of luck. He has reached the glass ceiling for fathers in child custody.

The Family Court System Is Biased Against Mothers

Garland Waller

In the following selection, Garland Waller argues that mothers are often denied custody of their children because judges, who are often male, are biased in favor of fathers. According to Waller, in cases where mothers make claims against their partners of physical and sexual abuse, judges often take the side of the fathers. She asserts that this is because judges believe that the abuse allegations are merely a part of the mother's attempt to disparage the father in hopes of alienating the children from the father and strengthening the mother's custody claims. To fix the family court system, Waller recommends that courtrooms be opened to the public to make judges more accountable. She also urges that child abuse allegations be taken seriously in every case.

Waller is a professor at Boston University in the College of Communication and an award-winning producer-writer-director of nationally syndicated and local television and film programs. She is currently producing an independent documentary with the working title of Small Justice: Little Justice in America's Family Courts.

Studies show that in approximately 70 percent of challenged cases, battering parents have been able to convince authorities during custody battles that their victim is unfit or undeserving of sole custody, according to a recent report published by the American Judges Foundation.

That statement would have once shocked me, but no more. Nor am I surprised when I read that a family court judge has awarded custody of a 3-year-old girl to the father who has

Garland Waller, "Biased Family Court System Hurts Mothers," *Women's E-News*, www.womensenews.org, September 5, 2001. Reproduced by permission.

violently beaten her mother. I do not even lift an eyebrow when a 2-year-old boy, who comes home from unsupervised visitation with his dad, has a diaper filled with his own rectal blood, and that same child is later turned over to his father on a full-time basis. And when a mother is thrown into jail, denied the right to ever see her children again, because she brought up the issue of child abuse in a family court, I'm sickened, but not shocked.

Abuse Ignored

These injustices are commonplace today in the closed-door family court system. These courts often claim to operate in a manner consistent with the "best interests of the child." In practice this often means that a judge, often a male judge, biased and imperious, defines that phrase. These judges decide, time and time again, when a woman raises the allegation of sexual abuse in a custody dispute, that it is she who will lose her children forever.

I used to think that the family court system was basically fair. That was before my childhood friend, Diane Hofheimer, asked me to consider doing a documentary on the family courts. She had taught herself the law so that she could work with her attorney husband, Charlie Hofheimer, in their Virginia law practice.

Representing only women in divorce and custody cases, Diane and Charlie began my education with one grisly case. I thought it was a fluke, but I agreed to look at some of the legal documents. And so began my journey into the dark world of family courts.

Children Put in Harm's Way

What I learned was that thousands of women are losing custody of their children to men with histories of violence and sexual abuse. Sure, these cases are complicated, but it doesn't take a legal genius to figure out that it's not good for kids to watch daddy break mommy's jaw. Research shows a high correlation between domestic violence and child sexual abuse.

"We have created a system that purports to be a gatekeeper—keeping victims from victimizers—but the system is really the welcome mat for victimizers to have access to the victims," says Richard Ducote, a nationally recognized child advocate and attorney. He adds that there has been virtually no change in the process during the past two decades.

In fact, a pilot study in the early 1990s by the California Protective Parent Association and Mothers of Lost Children found that 91 percent of fathers who were identified by their children as perpetrators of sexual abuse received full or partial unsupervised custody of the children and that in 54 percent of cases the non-abusing mother was placed on supervised visitation.

Parental Alienation Syndrome

One primary reason for what many consider a disastrous outcome, Ducote and other experts say, is the popularity of the theories of Dr. Richard Gardner, whose ideas are apparently more persuasive to judges than the testimony of battered women and victimized children.

Gardner's brainchild is Parental Alienation Syndrome. This is the name given for the practice of one parent saying disparaging things about the other parent in an attempt to alienate the child from the ex-spouse. This so-called syndrome is based on anecdotal evidence. Gardner's books on the subject are self-published, something that should give judges and experts pause, even though he does look good on paper.

He's a professor at Columbia Medical School and has been publishing papers for two decades. Fathers' rights groups love him.

Not addressed by Dr. Gardner and his adherents are what a mother should say to a child raped by her father. They merely discount all such allegations as examples of parental alienation syndrome, or some variation of it under a different name such as SAID (Sexual Allegations in Divorce) Syndrome, Malicious Mother Syndrome or some other fabricated condition.

These experts are certainly free to believe whatever they wish to, but much to the harm of thousands of children and their caring, protective parents, these ideas have been accepted by personnel in most of the family courts in the country: the judges, court-appointed lawyers charged with protecting the child's interests, and custody evaluators such as psychologists and social workers.

In essentially every case in which courts place children with abusers, despite substantial evidence of sexual abuse or domestic violence and no evidence of fabrication on the protecting parent's part, it is the parental alienation syndrome that is used by the judge, the evaluator or the child's lawyer to ignore and discount the abuse evidence and to wrongfully construe all of the child's symptoms as evidence of alienation.

Mothers Wrongly Blamed

My colleague Hofheimer is convinced that the so-called syndrome is to psychology what voodoo is to surgery.

"What would a good mother do," I asked Dr. Gardner two years ago when interviewing him for the documentary, "if her child told her of sexual abuse by his or her father?"

His answer: "What would she say? Don't you say that about your father. If you do, I'll beat you."

That's on tape and I have a signed release.

In researching my documentary, I have met many honest, caring and courageous mothers who, for speaking the truth, have been publicly called crazy, hysterical and delusional, and labeled with all kinds of pseudo-disorders for being strong and for fighting for the safety of their children.

Yet some of them have been nearly broken by the family court system, and the damage to their children is immeasurable. We must act now to begin reforming our family courts.

Recommendations

- Open the courtrooms to the public and make judges accountable for their rulings.

- Get rid of the "best interests of the child" as the standard for custody and replace it with a new concept called the "approximation standard." That means that the judge should try to approximate the same setup for the children that existed before the divorce. If mom was with the kids 70 percent of the time before the divorce, she would be with them 70 percent of the time after the divorce. In non-contested custody cases, the mother and father generally agree to this on their own.

- Most significantly, the allegation of child abuse in a custody battle must be considered a rebuttable presumption; that is, that the sworn testimony of a parent or child claiming abuse is presumed to be true unless and until the accused sufficiently challenges its veracity.

Divorce Is Always Damaging to Children

Elizabeth Marquardt

In the following selection, Elizabeth Marquardt attempts to debunk some of the most well known research on divorce that claims that children of divorce recover from the trauma and do not suffer lasting effects. She does this by reflecting on her experiences and the experiences of other now-adult children of divorce. Unlike some experts, she does not believe that there is any such thing as a "good divorce." To her, all divorces are damaging to children no matter how amicable. Marquardt is an affiliate scholar at the Institute for American Values and is the author of a number of publications, including Between Two Worlds: The Inner Lives of Children of Divorce, *from which this selection is excerpted.*

When I was growing up, divorce was an all-but-nonexistent topic of conversation. Beyond my own siblings I knew few other children of divorce; much less did I have any sense that I was part of a brand-new cohort, a generation of children marked by the first era of widespread divorce. I did, however, always feel "different" as a child; in the lingo of the seventies I thought of myself as a "weirdo." But I assumed my weirdness was part of who I was. Sometimes I took pride in it, but more often I felt lonely because of it.

It was only in my early twenties that I began to understand how common the experience of having divorced parents was. Only then did I begin to wonder how divorce might have shaped me as a person. I was born in 1970, just as the no-fault divorce revolution started sweeping the country. California was the first state to pass such legislation, in 1969, and virtually all the other states followed. My own parents, high-school sweethearts who were among the top graduates of their class in a small town in North Carolina, married in their first year of college, had me in their sophomore year, and separated when I was two years old. . . .

In some ways I was a fortunate child of divorce: I could take both parents' love for granted. So many like me lose a warm relationship with their father or lose that relationship entirely. The trouble was that I missed my mother and father terribly when I was separated from one of them—and I was always separated from one of them.

As a result of my parents' divorce, my childhood was filled with constant movement. I traveled often between my parents, spending school years with my mother and long summers, holiday breaks, and occasional weekends with my father. Even when I stayed in one place, other people did not. My childhood was routinely peopled with new faces—parents' boyfriends and girlfriends, new spouses, step- and half-siblings—that came and too often went.

The two people I loved the most and looked to as the rocks on which my own identity was built, my mother and my father, lived completely separate lives a six-hour drive apart. As I entered young adulthood I began to sense that growing up with parents in two different worlds, with me traveling between them, had shaped me in profound ways. I started to read avidly about divorce, looking for an explanation.

What We Do Know About Children of Divorce

I learned a lot from the studies I read about children of divorce, but there always seemed to be something missing. Most books and articles focus on the social or economic consequences of divorce, often showing the links between divorce and serious childhood problems such as poverty, dropping out of school, juvenile delinquency, early sexual activity, and teen pregnancy. For example, a . . . study by a major researcher, E. Mavis Hetherington, examined more than a thousand divorced families over three decades and found that 20 to 25 percent of young adults from divorced families experience "long-term damage"—serious social and emotional problems—compared to 10 percent of young people from intact families.

These kinds of studies are valuable. Learning how many children of divorce struggle with truly debilitating problems ought to make us question our society's high rate of divorce. I know some of these young people, and my heart goes out to them. Yet studies such as these are something of a blunt instrument; they capture only the most dramatic negative effects of divorce on children. As far as I could tell, I was not struggling with those kinds of problems, yet I suspected that divorce had still deeply influenced who I was.

Among all the researchers, Judith Wallerstein has been a pioneer in examining the more subtle psychological effects of divorce in children and young people. By getting to know a sample of children of divorce extremely well and returning again and again over the years to talk with them, Wallerstein has painted a detailed and sensitive portrait of the way divorce shapes the inner lives of many children, whether or not they end up with severe, diagnosable symptoms. For instance, her most recent book shows that experiencing parental divorce during childhood has a "sleeper effect": its worst symptoms often appear when children of divorce leave home and attempt to form intimate relationships and families of their own, but do so with much less ability to trust and little idea of what a lasting marriage looks like.

But there is an enormous story left untold. Although the number of divorces stabilized in this country in the early 1980s, close to half of first marriages still end in divorce. Today, one-quarter of all young adults in this country between the ages of eighteen and thirty-five have experienced the divorce of their parents. Many people look around and see plenty of young people from divorced families who seem just fine. These children of divorce graduate from high school and even college or beyond, get jobs, get married, have kids of their own. They are everywhere. If divorce causes such serious problems, then how do we explain these young people? . . .

Understanding the Impact of Divorce

The national debate about divorce has generally focused on the worst outcomes, with many assuming there is no need to worry about the children of divorce who appear to be fine. But I can think of few other significant childhood experiences that our society treats in the same way. Many people survive wrenching childhood traumas—child abuse, war, an alcoholic or drug-addicted parent—and nevertheless manage to become productive members of society. Yet no one would suggest that because they have survived the ordeal and now look "fine," their experience of child abuse, war, or addiction was apparently not that bad. On the contrary, our society sympathizes with these young people. It takes active steps to try to help them and to prevent other children, whenever possible, from growing up the same way.

Further, when our society asks only if a child has been hurt, and nothing more, it sets a very low bar for its expectations about children's lives. I'm a mother now. When I first held my daughter did I hope only that she would grow up and not be damaged? Of course not. Like all parents, my husband and I want to protect our children from suffering, but we also want them to thrive, to enjoy rich, loving relationships and have happy, successful futures. Parents do not set a low bar for their children, and neither should our society. Our society must do more than ask whether divorce causes clear and lasting damage to some children. It should also ask probing questions about how divorce shapes the lives of many children who experience it.

Just as most debates about children of divorce focus on the gravest and most obvious outcomes, most discussions about life in divorced families focus on the hot-button issue of conflict. When researchers examine how children fare in divorced families, many of them want to know how well or how poorly the divorced parents get along. Do they battle over custody of the child? Can they be in the same room together without getting into a fight? Are they able to stick to agreements on visitation and child support?

Learning more about the conflicts between divorced parents is undeniably important. But an overriding emphasis on the issue of conflict has led to a troubling idea that has quickly gained credibility in our culture. In recent years, some experts have speculated that if couples divorce amicably and if both parents continue to share in raising the child, then perhaps the negative effects of divorce can be avoided. Experts urge parents, for the sake of their children, to aim for what some call a "good divorce."

The Myth of the "Good Divorce"

The idea of the "good divorce" is attractive to many. Some divorced parents are reassured because it suggests steps they can take to try to protect their children if they must end a very bad marriage. Other parents like the idea of a "good divorce" because it suggests they can end a marriage that may be okay but not completely satisfying and still do right by their children. Family court judges welcome it because they want to make arrangements that, whenever possible, keep both parents in the child's life, and they want to minimize conflict between those parents. Some therapists like the idea because they want to help these families, and a "good divorce" gives them a role in teaching parents how to divorce. In addition, many social observers, including journalists, academics, and opinion leaders, like the idea of the "good divorce" because it promises to alleviate much of the anxiety our society has about divorce. What really matters, the experts assure us, is how the parents get along after the divorce, not the divorce itself.

References to the "good divorce"—and the idea behind it, that the quality of the divorce matters as much as, if not more than, the divorce itself—are everywhere. A therapist is quoted in the *Christian Science Monitor*, "A lot of times it's not the divorce itself that bothers children, but the level of conflict, or being caught in the middle." An academic expert opines, "Rather than discourage divorce per se, we, as a society, need to encourage more humane divorce." Another expert writes in a book review, "The problem is not so much with divorce itself but with the different ways men, women and children experience divorce and react to it." A holiday article in *Newsweek*, titled "Happy Divorce," features divorced families who put their conflicts aside in order to spend Christmas together as a family. It says that researchers "have known for years that *how* parents divorce matters even more than the divorce itself."

A November 2002 cover story in the *Washington Post Magazine* is titled "The Good Divorce: One Couple's Attempt to Split Up Without Tearing the Kids Apart." The cover photograph features a handsome, smiling, divorced family with three girls. Inside we learn about Debbie and Eli. Although their marriage was, according to Debbie, "all in all, an incredibly functional marriage," they divorced when she became troubled by their "lack of connection." The journalist is impressed that Eli, who Debbie agrees is a great father, still comes to Debbie's house each school morning to get the girls ready after she's left for work, as he has since they split three years previously. Eli says he shows up every morning to reassure his kids "that even though Mommy and Daddy aren't married, we're still your parents, we're still there for you and we still love you." Readers of the story might easily assume that the present arrangement will last until the girls leave home.

Yet as any child who has lived it will tell you, an arrangement like that of Eli and Debbie is inherently unstable and any number of events could spell its demise. What will happen when Eli or Debbie remarries? Will the new spouse feel happy about Eli showing up at Debbie's house every morning to get the girls ready for school? What happens when one of them begins dating? Will they still want their girls to pop in unannounced? What happens if Debbie gets a great job offer on the West Coast? Will she turn it down so that her ex-husband can continue dropping by for breakfast every morning?

Setting Up Rules

Another genre of "good divorce" news articles features tips and tools to help parents manage their divorce. Several recent articles trumpeted a new website—OurFamilyWizard.com— that is supposed to help divorced parents improve the quality of their communication. At the website each parent can make entries on a shared calendar, message board, data bank, and expense account. The site was created by one divorced dad to help deal with the "chaos" of managing multiple children's schedules in two families. But one journalist says, "Those involved in family law immediately recognized it for its value in the truly nasty cases—the ones where the parents can't get on the phone without the conversation devolving into a screaming match." The tone of articles such as these is always upbeat, with those interviewed expressing great confidence that if the adults will simply get better organized and play by the rules, then the children's pain following their parents' divorce will be greatly reduced.

Each time the "good divorce" is featured in a news article, it is greeted with fanfare and treated as a brand-new idea, one that gives no quarter to moralistic worrywarts who fret about the effects of divorce on children. Yet the idea of the "good divorce" has actually been around for more than a decade. The term was first coined by Constance Ahrons in 1994 when she published *The Good Divorce: Keeping Your Family Together When Your Marriage Comes Apart*. In that book Ahrons says that it is possible for couples to achieve a "good divorce" by setting clear rules governing postdivorce interactions. These rules prevent unnecessary conflict and allow both divorced parents to stay actively involved in the children's lives. If parents can achieve a "good divorce" they will have not a damaged divorced family but rather a thriving "binuclear" family—another term that Ahrons coins—and the children will be fine.

An Adult-Centered View

The premise of the "good divorce" sounds logical. Surely, if divorce does happen, it is better for children not to lose significant relationships entirely, nor to be drawn into bitter, unending fights. However, when you talk to the children themselves you find that the popular idea behind the "good divorce" —that the quality of the divorce matters more than the divorce itself—is actually an adult-centered vision that does not reflect their true experiences.

While a "good divorce" is better than a bad divorce, it is still not *good*. For no matter how amicable divorced parents might be and how much they each love and care for the child, their willingness to do these things does absolutely *nothing* to diminish the radical restructuring of the child's universe.

When Dr. Norval Glenn and I compared young adult children of divorce with their peers from intact families, we found that for children a "good divorce" often compares poorly even to an unhappy marriage, so long as that marriage is low-conflict (as approximately two-thirds of marriages that end in divorce are). Increasingly, too, many people think that a "good divorce" and a happy intact marriage are about the same for kids. As one observer reflected, "A good divorce, a good marriage, it matters not." But our research demonstrates strongly that, without question, a "good divorce" is far worse for children than a happy marriage. Of course, any child could tell you the same thing. No child thinks a "good divorce" is as good as the happy marriage of his or her own two parents.

How Divorce Changes Childhood

To grasp the reality of the lives of children of divorce we could not simply ask, as so many other researchers have, how many children of divorce end up with severe, tragic problems. We had to ask: How do children of divorce make sense of their parents' different beliefs, values, and ways of living when their parents no longer must confront these differences themselves? How do the feelings of loss and loneliness, so widespread in the lives of children of divorce, affect their spiritual journeys? How might divorce divide and shape the inner lives of many children, even those who appear to be successful later in life?

These questions may sound utterly natural but they are entirely new. Even the great works on children's moral and spiritual development either were written before divorce was widespread or ignore the fact of divorce and assume that all children still grow up with their own, married parents. . . .

Most children cannot conceive of keeping important secrets for their parents, but divorce required us to keep secrets routinely, even when our parents did not ask us to. Most children observe their parents confronting each other about their conflicting values and beliefs; sometimes these confrontations end in fights, sometimes in agreement, sometimes in stalemate. But the majority of those from divorced families say that as the years passed, our divorced parents did *not* have a lot of conflicts. Instead, we experienced something much deeper and more pernicious. The divorce left us with a permanent inner conflict between our parents' worlds. This was a conflict for which we could imagine no resolution, a conflict for which many of us thought we had only ourselves to blame.

For children of divorce, the idea that childhood is an important, protected time of spiritual growth is thrown into question as well. Many, if not most, parents feel that handing core religious or spiritual values on to their children is important. Yet children of divorce more often say that if we have strong spiritual beliefs it is something we came to *alone*, as a reaction to what was missing in our family life rather than an affirmation of it. We love our parents, but the idea that, for instance, God could be like a parent can be as foreboding as it is enticing, beckoning us to a spiritual life or alienating us from faith and spirituality for years to come. And this is only the beginning.

Divorce Is Not Always Damaging to Children

Karen S. Peterson

While most researchers acknowledge that divorce can be devastating for children, they have also come to see that it does not automatically guarantee a substandard future. In the following viewpoint Karen Peterson discusses the findings of researcher E. Mavis Hetherington, many of which are in opposition to earlier studies measuring the lifelong impact of divorce on kids. Hetherington finds that the overwhelming majority of children from divorced families are "functioning in the normal range," and successfully going about the business of becoming young adults. Hetherington does acknowledge that she is not "pro-divorce," but knowing that not all marriages will last, her research dispels the notion that divorce inevitably results in a bad outcome for the children involved. Karen Peterson is a writer for USA Today.

A new, book-length study to be published this month [January 2002] says that the negative impact of divorce on both children and parents has been exaggerated and that only about one-fifth of youngsters experience any long-term damage after their parents break up. One of the most comprehensive studies of divorce to date, the research will bring balm to the souls of parents who have chosen to end their marriages. It probably also will incense those who see divorce as undermining American society.

After studying almost 1,400 families and more than 2,500 children—some of them for three decades—trailblazing researcher E. Mavis Hetherington finds that about 75% to 80% of children from divorced homes are "coping reasonably well and functioning in the normal range." Eventually they are able to adapt to their new lives.

About 70% of their parents are leading lives that range from "good enough"—the divorce was "like a speed bump in the road"—to "enhanced," living lives better than those they had before the divorce.

About 70% of kids in stepfamilies are "pretty happy," Hetherington says. And 40% of couples in stepfamilies were able to build "stable, reasonably satisfying marriages." . . .

Much of the current writing about divorce, both popular and academic, "has exaggerated its negative effects and ignored its sometimes considerable positive effects," Hetherington writes.

Ending a marriage, she says, "is an experience that for most people is challenging and painful. But it is also a window of opportunity to build a new and better life."

The Gold Standard of Research

Hetherington, whose research methods are regarded by her peers as the gold standard, is professor emeritus in the department of psychology at the University of Virginia. She writes: The vast majority of children within two years after their parents' divorce "are beginning to function reasonably well again." Most young adults from divorced families were "behaving the way young adults were supposed to behave, choosing careers, developing permanent relationships, ably going about the central tasks of young adulthood." . . .

Just how much damage divorce does to kids is a real hot-button topic. Hetherington's findings contradict those of several renowned experts who say the children are at risk for a variety of difficulties, including dropping out of school, emotional problems, substance abuse, having babies out of wedlock and having their own marriages end in divorce.

Over the past decade, researchers highlighting such results have dominated the public deliberations, leading some state legislatures to debate changes in divorce laws.

Hetherington now steps in, hoping to alter the national dialogue. The country has been so caught up in believing that the long-term effects of divorce are inevitably harmful that it is almost becoming a self-fulfilling prophecy, Hetherington says. "I think it is really important to emphasize that most do cope and go on to have a reasonably happy or sometimes very happy life," she says.

She adds a caveat. To ensure an emotionally healthy youngster, "there must be a competent, caring parent," she says.

The 75-year-old developmental psychologist—she volunteers her age—does have credentials. She invented many of the in-depth tools now commonly used to measure well-being in families, producing a nuanced look at what happens in divorce. And she has a control group of intact families for much of her work, so she can make comparisons with the normal troubles non-divorced families encounter.

That control group, the size of her sample, the length of time she has gathered data and the thoroughness of her work awe her peers. "She is the leading social scientist who studies the effects of divorce on children," says Andrew Cherlin, a sociologist at Johns Hopkins University in Baltimore. "She was the pioneer in her field, and we have all followed in her wake. She was the first serious researcher to do excellent, rigorous studies of children and families. Everyone has read her work and learned from it."

Family historian Stephanie Coontz, co-chairman of the Council on Contemporary Families, says Hetherington is "the perfectly balanced scholar. She is absolutely respected among her peers. Her advice is as good as you are going to get."

Seated in her 100-year-old home, a renovated schoolhouse overlooking the Blue Ridge mountains, Hetherington elaborates on her incendiary goal: altering the national debate. Her voice takes on a slightly sharp edge. She does not believe that divorce is all right. "I am saying it is painful," she says.

But it is also true that the disastrous results of splitting up have been exaggerated for both children and parents. A lot of people believe that "if you have gone through a divorce, you are inflicting a terminal disease on your children," she says.

Few criticize Hetherington outright. But even as many tip their hats to her, the disapproving already are lining up.

David Blankenhorn, one skeptic, is the author of *Fatherless America* and a leader of the growing "marriage movement," which seeks to reduce the number of marriages that end in divorce.

Hetherington's book will stoke "a sort of backlash," Blankenhorn says. "We have made so much progress in the last 10 years in what I would call realism about divorce. Reputable scholars have led a trend away from a kind of 'happy talk' approach to divorce. Even the title of her book says something: that we are reconsidering divorce, the fact that divorce is harmful to children." He takes issue with those like Hetherington who believe, he says, that "we shouldn't worry so much" or that "the kids will be fine." . . .

Linda Waite, sociologist at the University of Chicago and co-author of the *Case for Marriage*, questions one of Hetherington's key findings, that perhaps the surest way for a child of divorce to avoid a divorce himself is to marry someone from an intact family. "Then what she is really saying is that if you are a divorced person, nobody should marry your child," Waite says. . . .

Still, most children of divorce make it through. Rather than thinking about "the inevitability of any one kind of outcome of divorce," Hetherington hopes readers think about the "diversity of outcomes. What is striking is that we go from those who are totally defeated, mired in depression and poverty, to these ebullient, happy, satisfied people making wonderful contributions to their families and society." . . .

Not "Pro-divorce"

Hetherington has been married 46 years and has three grown sons and three grandchildren. Neither she nor her sons have ever been divorced.

And she would like to make one thing perfectly clear. "The last thing I want to do is sound like I am recommending divorce. I am not pro-divorce. I think people should work harder on their marriages and be better prepared when they go in and more willing to weather out the rough spots and support each other."

But divorce, she says, "is a legitimate decision. If children are in marriages with parents who are contemptuous of each other, not even with overt conflict, but just sneering and subtle putdowns that erode the partner's self-esteem, that is very bad for kids."

Children of Divorce Have Higher Rates of Divorce

Nicholas H. Wolfinger

Multiple studies have found that children of divorced parents are more likely to have their own marriages end in divorce than are children whose families remained intact. It is a phenomenon researchers have labeled the "divorce cycle." In the following selection, Nicholas H. Wolfinger argues that the divorce cycle is perpetuated in part because of marriage timing and partner selection. He also found that if both spouses' parents divorced, then the couple is 200 percent more likely to divorce as well. Wolfinger notes, however, that increases in the divorce rate have decreased the negative social ramifications of divorce, which is leading to a decline in the divorce rate among children of divorce. He concludes that while the divorce rate remains high for children of divorce, they have a better chance than ever of maintaining long-lasting marriages. Wolfinger is a professor of Family and Consumer Sciences at the University of Utah and is coeditor of the book Fragile Families and the Marriage Agenda.

The divorce cycle is an integral part of the demographic landscape in contemporary America. Growing up in a divorced family greatly increases the chances that one's own marriage will end in divorce. Although the magnitude of the increase varies, it is reasonable to say that compared to people who did not come from divorced families, experiencing parental divorce increases the chances of ending one's own marriage by at least 50 percent.

Over the past few decades, researchers have demonstrated that gender, religion, race, and socioeconomic origins have

Nicholas H. Wolfinger, *Understanding the Divorce Cycle: The Children of Divorce in Their Own Marriages*. New York: Cambridge University Press, 2005. Copyright © 2005 Cambridge University Press. Reprinted with the permission of Cambridge University Press.

considerable ability to explain social behavior. As a phenomenon with implications for the social sciences, the divorce cycle is extraordinarily powerful, because it operates largely irrespective of all these demographic influences: Parental divorce affects members of different groups the same way. Moreover, family structure of origin is a stronger predictor of offspring marital stability than are religion, race, or socioeconomic background.

These are significant results given the ubiquity of divorce in contemporary America. About 40 percent of children will grow up in divorced families; hence, many millions of adults will experience the effects of divorce on their own marital behavior in profound ways. . . .

Marriage Timing

Evidence of the divorce cycle begins early in the life course. Parental divorce increases the incidence of premature teenage sexual activity, which in turn leads to teenage marriage. Another reason the children of divorce have high rates of teenage marriage is their desire to escape unhappy home lives. At age eighteen, for instance, 1994 General Social Survey (GSS) respondents from divorced families have marriage rates 27 percent higher than their peers from intact families. Generally, teenagers in stepfamilies have marriage rates about 20 percent higher than do those whose divorced parents did not remarry. The effect of parental divorce on offspring marital behavior diminishes as the children of divorce leave their teens, so that by age twenty the children of divorce have marriage rates comparable to people from intact families.

The relationship between parental divorce and teenage marriage has important implications for marital stability. Other things being equal, a couple with a mean marriage age of twenty is 32 percent less likely to divorce than a couple with a mean marriage age of eighteen. Most teenagers are not ready for a commitment as serious and potentially enduring as matrimony. The longer they wait, the more likely they are to develop the social and inner resources necessary to succeed in their marriages. The propensity for youthful wedlock therefore contributes to the difficulties the children of divorce face in their own marriages, although it is far from being the most important cause of the divorce cycle. People who delay marriage also are more likely to graduate from college. Youthful marriage often forces newlyweds into the work force or into duty as homemakers.

If the children of divorce do not marry by age twenty, the likelihood of their ever marrying dips about 30 percent below that of their peers from intact families. Growing up in a divorced family often leaves offspring ambivalent about marriage. Many opt for cohabitation, a form of intimate relationship offering some of the same benefits of marriage but not entailing the same commitment or risk.

This is a mixed blessing. Cohabitation inherently is a less stable form of union than matrimony, with lower levels of partner satisfaction. On the other hand, judging by their high divorce rates, some people from divorced families may not be suited for marriage. If they cohabit instead, they spare themselves, their partners, and possibly their children the upheaval of divorce. Finally, it should not be forgotten that many people who cohabit will eventually marry each other. Parental divorce plays a role here too. . . .

Mate Selection

Parental divorce affects not only the decision to marry but the kinds of people chosen as spouses. In particular, the children of divorce often marry other children of divorce, a phenomenon I have called family structure homogamy. Compared to people from intact families, the children of divorce are about 50 percent more likely to choose a spouse from a divorced family. This helps explain the divorce cycle, given that marriages between people from divorced families are more likely to fail than are unions involving only one child of divorce.

Even more than the divorce cycle itself, family structure homogamy affects everybody the same way, transcending barriers of gender, race, religion, and to a large extent social class. Variations in family structure such as parental remarriage and multiple parental divorces have no effect on the chances of choosing a spouse from a divorced family. The only personal characteristic that affects family structure homogamy is education. People with college degrees are considerably less likely to marry the children of divorce, a result that probably can be explained on the basis of marriage markets. Parental divorce decreases the chances of attending college. Thus the children of divorce are underrepresented on any given college campus, while many people who attend college will meet their future spouses there. This reduces the likelihood that college graduates will marry people from divorced families. Even after accounting for differences in education, the children of divorce are likely to marry other children of divorce, so college attendance plays only a partial role in explaining the relationship between parental background and partner selection.

More generally, family structure homogamy tells us something important about the long-term consequences of family breakdown. Parental divorce clearly has far-reaching effects on offspring if such a broad demographic variable—family structure—can exert such a great influence on something so deeply personal: the kind of person one chooses to marry. . . . Although the psychological mechanisms responsible for the divorce cycle are fairly well understood, it is not clear why people from divorced families are so likely to marry other children of divorce. Perhaps in-depth clinical interviews or survey data with detailed psychometric information could shed light on the subject.

What Makes the Divorce Cycle Stronger or Weaker?

Family structure homogamy helps explain the divorce cycle. If both spouses come from divorced families, the marriage be comes over 200 percent more likely to fail than a marriage be-tween people who did not grow up in divorced families. This result accords with the finding that divorce transmission can be attributed to reduced marital commitment. It makes sense that a marriage where both spouses exhibit low commitment is more likely to fail than a union where only one or neither spouse exhibits reduced commitment. In colloquial terms, there simply is less glue to hold the relationship together. This is important to keep in mind given the high likelihood that the children of divorce will marry each other.

Another important variable affecting the strength of di-vorce transmission concerns the number of family structure transitions children undergo while growing up. Other things being equal, the rate of divorce transmission increases with each disruption. The divorce cycle is set into motion initially when a child experiences divorce. The chances that the child will end a marriage increase considerably with parental remar-riage, while a second parental divorce increases the probability even more. . . .

Because they strengthen the message children receive about low commitment, multiple transitions while growing up in-crease the likelihood of divorce transmission. A child who ex-periences one divorce may learn that marriage need not last forever. After a second divorce, the message becomes clearer. Stepparenting probably reinforces this message by suggesting that spouses can be replaced.

This last point is speculative. Most studies have shown that remarriage exacerbates the negative effects of parental di-vorce (or at the very least has no impact on children), so the results described here accord with previous research on the consequences of stepparenting. Moreover, the effects of step-parenting on offspring marital behavior can easily be inter-preted within the framework established by the "low commit-ment" explanation for the divorce cycle: The presence of a stepparent shows children that divorce does not mean forever forsaking marriage. Perhaps for this reason, offspring raised in stepfamilies have even higher divorce rates than do people raised in single-parent divorced families.

Multiple transitions while growing up affect second and third marriages as well as initial unions. This finding is interesting for two reasons. First, the children of divorce do not change their marital behavior as a result of their experiences in their initial marriages; the adverse consequences of parental divorce apparently manifest themselves in all of one's conjugal relationships. Second, people's marital behavior mirrors their childhood experiences. The more marital transitions children experience, the more marriages they are likely to dissolve as adults. This provides a useful template for understanding the divorce cycle, and perhaps other patterns of adult behavior that occur consequent to growing up in a divorced family. It also is evidence for a fundamentally simple understanding of human behavior: We repeat what we learn in our youth.

Parental divorce affects offspring marital behavior largely irrespective of social differences between offspring and their families of origin. Parental socioeconomic characteristics—education, occupation, history of receiving public aid—as well as offspring marriage timing account for a small portion of the relationship between growing up in a divorced family and one's own marital stability. Perhaps the most important demographic variable affecting the divorce cycle is education, given the effect of parental divorce on educational attainment and the strong correlation between education and marital stability. Combined, parental socioeconomic status, respondent education, marriage age, and other demographic differences between people from divorced and intact families account for at best one-third of the divorce cycle. Most of the remainder is attributable . . . to the effects of parental divorce on marital functioning and commitment.

The "black box" explanation for divorce transmission is genetics, but its role in the divorce cycle cannot be ascertained with the data at hand. It could not be preponderant, though, given that the divorce cycle has many nonbiological determinants. If the divorce cycle were completely attributable to genetics, social differences between respondents (such as education or the presence of stepparents) would not produce different levels of divorce transmission. Genetics also cannot explain why the negative effects of parental divorce have weakened over time.

Historical Trends

Increases in the divorce rate have diminished the negative consequences of coming from a divorced family. Two phenomena have been affected: the divorce cycle itself; and the association between family background and marriage timing.

Teenagers from divorced families still have higher marriage rates than do teenagers from intact families, but the gap narrowed between 1973 and 1994. The most likely explanation for this trend concerns the changing circumstances under which people choose to divorce. In the absence of no-fault divorce laws, couples needed greater justification to obtain a divorce. When couples finally ended their marriages, the situation may have deteriorated much further than is typical in most modern divorces. It is impossible to know for certain whether only the very worst marriages were dissolved in years gone by. But if we accept this proposition, it follows that children used to be exposed to far more conflict than is typical in most modern divorces. One reason that teenagers from divorced families married was to escape unpleasant home environments. If parental divorce is less unpleasant than it used to be, teenagers may feel less pressure to escape through marriage. This could explain why their marriage rates have been lower in recent years. . . .

Past age twenty, the children of divorce now have lower overall marriage rates, whereas thirty years ago the opposite was true. The most likely explanation for this development is the increased acceptability of cohabitation as an alternative to matrimony. Growing up in a divorced family often reduces children's faith in the institution of marriage, so they cohabit instead. As cohabitation grew more common, it became an increasingly appealing option for the children of divorce.

The declining rate of teenage marriage has contributed to the weakening of the divorce cycle. Since youthful marriage is a strong predictor of divorce, the children of divorce now fare better in their own marriages because they are less likely to wed as teenagers. General Social Survey [GSS] respondents from divorced single-parent families interviewed in 1973 were 126 percent more likely to have dissolved their own marriages than were people from intact families. By 1994, the disparity had declined to 45 percent. Controlling for age at marriage reduces the figures for 1973 and 1994 to 94 percent and 33 percent, respectively. The divorce cycle would have abated even if rates of teenage marriage had not declined, although changing patterns of marriage timing have had a substantial impact.

Rates of divorce transmission have not changed for people raised in stepfamilies. Between 1973 and 1994, GSS respondents experiencing both parental divorce and remarriage were 91 percent more likely to end their own marriages than were people from intact families.

The divorce cycle is primarily attributable to the effect of parental divorce on marital commitment, and the message children receive about commitment has almost certainly changed over time. If your parents were the only couple in the neighborhood to end their marriage—a fairly common situation prior to the 1960s—it conveyed a far more poignant lesson about the permanence of marital bonds than it does today. Children learned that marriage could be forsaken when it went sour, and that sometimes the best solution to marital difficulties was to cut one's losses and move on. In contrast, no matter how painful it is at the time, a modern divorce does not stand out against the experiences of one's peers, and therefore does not send nearly as strong a message to offspring about commitment. Surrounded by divorced families, today's children learn relatively similar lessons about marital commitment whether or not their own parents are divorced. As a result, people are now less likely to divorce as a result of growing up in a divorced family. The normalization of divorce, in short, means that it conveys a weaker message about marital commitment than it once did.

Lower Rates of Divorce Transmission

The declining stigma of growing up in a divorced family probably also has contributed to lower rates of divorce transmission. In the past, when divorces were few and far between, single mothers and their children were often viewed with both contempt and pity. Under these conditions, the children were less likely to develop normal relationships with their peers, relatives, and communities. This may have exacerbated the lessons children learned about marital commitment, given the powerful relationship between stigma and personal development, and increased their chances of having difficulty in their own marriages. . . .

Even if the reasons for the weakening in the divorce cycle cannot be verified, the implications are undeniable: Declines in the intergenerational transmission of divorce mean that millions of young Americans now face substantially lower odds of divorce in their own marriages than they would have, had the rates of divorce transmission remained constant. In addition, rates of teenage marriage for the children of divorce also have declined. Fewer teenage marriages by the children of divorce diminishes the number of at-risk unions, and should in itself contribute to lower divorce rates. Irrespective of whether they persist, these trends have transformed our demographic landscape for decades to come. All else being equal, a lower rate of divorce transmission in this generation means fewer divorces in the next.

CHAPTER 4

Personal Narratives
on Divorce

A Journey Through the Catholic Annulment Process

Joseph A. Califano Jr.

While divorce remains a very limited option for members of the Catholic Church, more and more Catholics are seeking annulments. An annulment, or a "declaration of nullity," is not the same as a legal or civil divorce; it is a church-sanctioned marriage dissolution. The church tribunal decrees that the marriage was never valid according to church doctrine. There are many ways in which prior marriages can be seen as invalid, including if the couple was wed under false pretenses and if one or both partners were previously married. Thought by some critics to be a sign of church hypocrisy, given its usually firm stance against divorce, others, like Joseph A. Califano Jr., have found that the annulment process brings them closer to their faith and religious community. Ten years after legally divorcing his first wife, Califano decided to pursue an annulment in the hopes of finding reconciliation and sacramental validation for his second marriage. In explaining the annulment process in the following selection, he dispels commonly held myths about the decree. Following the annulment, he and his second wife renewed their wedding vows in the church. He states that going through the process not only helped him make peace with his first wife, but it also further strengthened his relationship with his new family. A former U.S. secretary of health, education, and welfare, Joseph A. Califano Jr. is the president of the National Center on Addiction and Substance Abuse at Columbia University and the author of several books, including Inside: A Public and Private Life *and* America's Health Care Revolution: Who Lives, Who Dies, Who Pays.

Like many divorced and remarried Catholics, I looked down on the church's annulment process, viewing it as cover for Catholic divorce, a process tinged with hypocrisy, reserved for the rich and powerful.

Then one day, Walter Modrys, S.J. [Society of Jesus], my pastor at the Church of St. Ignatius Loyola in Manhattan, said to me: "You've mentioned several times you were not married in the Catholic Church. It obviously bothers you. Why don't you seek an annulment?"

"How can I do that? I was married 20 years before we separated. I've got three children."

"Don't be so sure," he said. "The church is understanding, especially if you were married young and didn't fully understand what marriage was all about. How old were you and your wife when you got married?"

"I was 24, she was 22."

"Think about it," he said.

With each passing year and the changes in American society, the church had become more important to me. As a Catholic, I was finding little support and reinforcement for my faith and values in our society, particularly in my milieu, New York City's Upper East Side and Ivy League academia. Popular films, television, books and the nation's style-setting institutions were becoming more aggressively secular. Our culture was materialistic and hedonistic. As the culture seemed to drift further from faith-based values, I found the church to be my most solid and reassuring rock.

An annulment would end any remaining estrangement from the church. But how, after 23 years, could there be a determination that there never was a marriage? How would my children, Mark, Joe and Claudia, react to having their parents' marriage annulled? Our divorce had not been easy for them. Ten years later, they were still puzzled, hurt and suffering emotionally from our breakup. Annulment would raise another issue for them: were they legitimate? My current wife,

Hilary, had two children; her daughter, Brooke, had become a devout Catholic. How would she react? I was concerned that my receiving an annulment would in some way undermine their faith and commitment to the church, which I considered my most important legacy to them. I hoped that Hilary's son, Frick, would someday receive the gift of faith. How would he take it? How would my former wife react?

The Annulment Process

Father Modrys suggested I see Amadeus McKevitt, O.S.U. [Order of St. Ursula], at the Metropolitan Tribunal of the Archdiocese of New York. I visited Sister Amadeus, and as I told her my doubts and how long I had been married, she gently interrupted. "The church seeks ways to have divorced and remarried Catholics fully integrated and to permit them to marry within the church. That's what I'm here for."

"What's important," she continued, "is whether you fully understood—or were capable of understanding—all the rights and obligations of marriage at the time you wed."

I was skeptical, but she was reassuring. The bond of marriage, she said, should contain "an efficacious grace," which is attached to all sacraments. "That grace enables the couple to raise children and love each other through good times and bad. The annulment process tries to determine if that sacramental grace was there at the beginning of a marriage and seeks to restore the possibility of that grace occurring in another marriage."

She explained that I would have to respond in writing to a rigorous series of questions. If grounds for annulment were based on psychological factors, which she believed mine would be, then a psychologist would examine me. Based on my application, the testimony of any witnesses and the psychologist's assessment, a determination would be made about whether there was sufficient reason to hold a formal hearing. If so, I would be asked to give sworn testimony before a canon law [church law] judge.

"Would my first wife and I face off against each other?" I asked.

"The annulment process is not adversarial," Sister Amadeus insisted. "What we seek is healing. An effort is always made to contact the other spouse. If your wife wants to testify, the judge will hear her privately, but she is not obligated."

Sister Amadeus stressed that the annulment process is of an entirely different character from divorce proceedings. "Although many call an annulment a 'Catholic divorce,'" she said, "it is not. It is differentiated from the civil process because the judges look only at the person you were, your maturity and understanding at the time of the wedding, your previous dating experience and your courtship. They do not focus on what went wrong during your marriage—though these facts often support the allegation of invalidity."

My mind was opening to a world of hope as I listened to this caring nun. "In fact, the annulment process can heal the scars of divorce," she added.

After testimony was taken, she said, the tribunal would consider the matter and make a decision. She explained that the tribunal consisted of a judge; a defender of the bond, who was responsible for marshalling and presenting the arguments against annulment; an advocate to present my case for annulment; and one for my former spouse, if she wished to participate.

Sister Amadeus then said, "Normally there is a charge, $600, to cover the tribunal's costs."

I was surprised the amount was so low, having heard stories that obtaining a Catholic annulment could involve a significant contribution to the church.

Seeing the surprise on my face, Sister Amadeus said, "For those who cannot pay all at once, we can work out installment payments. And if the parish priest tells us that an individual—say a single parent—cannot afford to pay anything, there is no charge."

This wonderful woman had misread my expression. "Sister," I said, "I am more than able to pay the $600. I was just surprised that it was so little."

Sister Amadeus suggested that I read a book, *Annulment: Your Chance to Remarry Within the Catholic Church*, by Joseph Zwack. I learned that for years the Catholic Church in the United States had considered psychological factors in determining the validity of the bond (and granted thousands of annulments on these grounds). Out of Pope John XXIII's Second Vatican Council came a revised Code of Canon Law, which included among those considered incapable of "matrimonial consent" individuals who "suffer from a grave lack of discretionary judgment concerning the essential matrimonial rights and obligations to be mutually given and accepted." The ability to grasp fully—not just intellectually, but emotionally and spiritually—and to assume the real obligations of a mature, lifelong commitment was a prerequisite to valid matrimonial consent. In the absence of such full understanding, the church could find that no valid marriage ever existed.

Working Through the Process

Once I decided to seek an annulment, I faced the prospect of telling my first wife and the children. My first wife expressed no surprise. I told her that at some point the tribunal would give her a chance to participate. She expressed little interest; and when contacted by the tribunal, she never responded.

Next I explained to each of my children individually how important it was to me to be married in the Catholic Church. Mark and Joe simply listened, as did Brooke. Claudia was concerned: Would this mean she was an illegitimate child? I explained that the ecclesiastical annulment had nothing to do with the fact that she was the legitimate and much-loved child of her mother and me. I suggested that she see Father Modrys, which she did. He put her at ease. In the end, I suspect all the children considered this the church's cover for divorce—that

Mark, Joe and Claudia didn't like it, but they were willing to accept whatever would make me happy.

With help from Sister Amadeus, I worked on my statement—a short biographical account of my background, upbringing, courtship and marriage. I noted that neither my first wife nor I had gone through any pre-Cana [premarital] preparation to gain an appreciation of the rights and obligations of marriage.

I went to the office of C. Edward Robins for an interview and psychological assessment. I entered gingerly, uncomfortable to be analyzed by a psychologist. His questions focused on my upbringing, parental relationships, courtship with my first wife and the early years of our married life.

One month later, I signed the petition for annulment, in which I appointed Rosemary Doherty of the Metropolitan Tribunal to be my "procurator advocate" and authorized her to represent me before the tribunal and the Court of Second Instance, the ecclesiastical body that would review the tribunal's decision. If the tribunal ruled in my favor and the ecclesiastical court agreed, the annulment would be granted. I never met Rosemary Doherty, but Sister Amadeus said she was an excellent advocate.

My petition was accepted, and a formal meeting was scheduled with Msgr. Desmond Vella, J.C.D [Doctor of Canon Law]. Monsignor Vella placed me under oath and tape-recorded my testimony. His questions centered on my understanding of the covenant of marriage when I entered into it, the lack of any preparation for marriage and the extent to which I appreciated—or failed to appreciate—the rights and obligations of marriage at the time. He asked pointed questions about my courtship and engagement and the early years of my marriage. He spoke in a firm, sometimes insistent, but invariably courteous way. I had entered his office on edge and nervous, but I left feeling gratitude for his thoroughness and courtesy.

Months later, I received word that an annulment had been granted. Hilary and I celebrated our church wedding at St. Ignatius Loyola, with Father Modrys officiating. I have rarely known such peace as I experienced that evening. There was a sense of integration with my church and within myself, a letting go of guilt and failure. The bond with Hilary has been immeasurably strengthened with sacramental grace.

Misunderstandings About Annulments

I have often thought about the stigma attached to annulments: that they were granted only to the biggest donors or most famous members of the church. In fact, during 1991, the year I began the annulment process, Catholic marriage tribunals in the United States heard nearly 40,000 cases and approved more than 90 percent of the petitions. Still, I took notice in 1997, when Sheila Rauch Kennedy published a scalding book, *Shattered Faith*, about the annulment of her marriage to Massachusetts congressman Joseph P. Kennedy II. She recounts a conversation in which she says she will oppose the annulment, and Joe Kennedy responds, "I don't believe this stuff. Nobody actually believes it. It's just Catholic gobbledygook, Sheila. But you just have to say it this way because, well, because that's the way the church is." It may be impossible for those outside the Catholic tradition—and for many within it—to understand, but my experience could not have been more different.

Most of my friends, and many if not most Catholics, think of the church's annulment process as some kind of mumbo jumbo, a sop to the large number of Catholics who have divorced and remarried, especially those with money or contacts in the church hierarchy—as did I until I experienced the process. To be sure, Catholic marriage tribunals and the annulment process they adjudicate are institutions set up by human beings, not by God, with the limitations and imperfections that attend any institution that seeks to accommodate human frailty. But they fill a real need of divorced and remarried Catholics committed to their faith.

Going through the spiritual, psychological and emotional process of reflection on my first marriage and why it did not work out, and then entering into a sacramental marriage with Hilary within my church, gave me a peace of mind and soul I have never before known. It is a peace that was so foreign to me I didn't even realize it was missing from my life. I have since felt at peace with my first wife as well. Though my children were not present at the ceremony, I believe that the spiritual peace of that event has spilled over into their lives and their relationship with Hilary and me. As Sister Amadeus promised, my marriage has been enriched by a penetrating infusion of sacramental grace that has deepened our commitment and love and touched all of our children, Hilary's as well as mine.

I told Sister Amadeus a decade later, "Sister, I still don't understand what motivated me to get an annulment in the first place and what's happened to me since."

"Maybe you'll never understand it," she said softly. "The fact is, you experienced it."

An Adult Daughter Struggles with Her Parents' Divorce

Brooke Lea Foster

Studies of the effects of divorce on families have primarily focused on young children and adolescents who suffer through their parents' breakup. Recently, however, new studies have emerged to illuminate the toll divorce takes on adult children. In the following selection, Brooke Lea Foster discusses the anguish she felt when her parents divorced when she was twenty-six years old. Acknowledging that adult children are often left out of discussions and research on the ramifications of divorce, Foster explains how the process is different for them than it is for young children. She says that their grief is not taken seriously, and others assume that they can easily overcome the emotional turmoil left in the wake of their parents' decisions. Unlike young children, adult children whose parents are divorcing are often expected to listen to details of their parents' breakup and must forge new relationships with their parents. In response to her anger and pain, she decided to reach out to other adult children of divorce by writing about her struggle in The Way They Were: Dealing with Your Parents' Divorce After a Lifetime of Marriage, *from which the following excerpt is taken. Foster is a staff writer for the District of Columbia magazine the* Washingtonian *and has had articles appear in* Parents *magazine and other publications.*

Nothing tested me more in my adult life than my parents' split. I can say that now without feeling embarrassed or weak. For a long time, that's all I felt. I was twenty-six years old at the time. I had moved out of my childhood home to attend college several years before. I was in a long-term relationship. I had a great job and a small circle of close friends. My parents weren't sick or dying. I had all of the things that should make you feel rooted. Yet, when my parents announced they were separating, I felt as if the world had collapsed in on me.

My age made everyone assume I'd be fine. Even I decided I was overreacting. I figured, *I'm an adult. I should be able to handle this*. So I felt guilty hurting so much, as if my grief were out of place or unwarranted. I'd curse myself if I lost control of my emotions. I figured I had no right to sit in my apartment bedroom with the door shut crying about my parents' divorce, mourning the way I did the time my dog ran away when I was seven years old—the kind of crying that takes away your breath like a bad case of the hiccups. I was bullying myself over my own tears.

My parents were separated several months before I told anyone with whom I was close, I feared friends would laugh at my grief. When I did confide in them, some said, "Better now than if you were a kid." Then I regretted saying anything at all.

There is an assumption that parental divorce won't hurt an adult child, that twenty-six- or thirty-five-year-olds aren't as likely to be affected by their parents' breakup. That they'll understand. After interviewing more than seventy-five adults whose parents divorced later in life, I can confidently say I'm not the only one struggling. Ninety percent of those surveyed said their parents' divorce was a defining moment in their lives. Nearly everyone felt as if their relationships with their parents had changed—sometimes for the better, more often for the worse. Many lost financial support, such as money for college. Lawyers drained inheritances. Adult children said they lost their sense of belonging. Divorce shattered their family and their concept of "home." Something inside of them died.

I envy young children going through a divorce. Everyone worries about them. They're sent to psychologists. Thousands of studies analyze their development through life. Dozens of books square off on how divorce impacts them. Parents go out of their way to ensure that a young child's transition is smooth. They're expected to hurt.

Adult kids aren't so lucky. Says one thirty-one-year-old woman, "If I could go back and tell my younger self what to expect, I think I would say, 'Just because you're almost thirty, don't feel like [your parents' divorce] shouldn't hurt. It will hurt like hell. In a way, it's harder for you than for a little kid. You've had thirty years for your parents' relationship to become part of your identity.'"

Different Concerns for Adult Children

Our grief isn't taken as seriously as a young child's. Our parents stayed together *because* we'd be more mature once we headed off to college, walked down the aisle, had our first baby. Parents expect us to shrug off their split, as if the breakup of our family should no longer concern us because pieces of our adult life are in place. My mother wasn't the only one who thought congratulations were in order. Parents take such a big step in separating, some expect their adult children to be proud. Therapists say parents are shocked when their grown children show distress.

Adult children struggle with divorce just as young children do, only we're old enough to understand what's going on. We can attach words to all of the changes. We take on caregiver roles, watching out for our parents in ways we're used to parents watching over us. We grow depressed trying to understand what the word *family* means now that ours is split apart. Our emotional development suspends. Finding lasting love can seem fruitless.

Yet adult children and young children experience our parents' divorces differently. No one covers the adult child's ears or lowers their voices if we walk into the room as family matters are discussed. Parents openly burden adult children with their problems, treating us like friends. On their own for the first time in twenty years or more, parents need guidance and support. We teach Dad how to do laundry and cook a red sauce. We counsel Mom on dating. Says one twenty-five-year-old woman of her divorcing parents, "I felt like we were all growing up together."

Expected to Be Adult Enough to Handle the Pain

If Dad cheats or Mom takes off with Dad's savings, adult children are the first to know. Parents forget that just because we're in our twenties doesn't mean we feel any less like their son or daughter. Hearing details of their problems—learning how miserable they've been—tears us apart inside. We have a personal stake in the loss. It's painful to listen to. Yet, as an older son or daughter, we're somehow expected to.

Divorce means watching the two people we love most turn against each other and sometimes try to destroy the other—and because we are adults, we are privy to every excruciating detail. Mom and Dad hire expensive lawyers. Sometimes they hide assets and lie. They push us to take sides, manipulating us with angry phone calls and emotional e-mails. Instead of sitting us down and explaining what's happening, as they would with a young child, parents suck us into the middle. They want us to hear about every jab and knockout punch they've exchanged. We cannot sit back like docile spectators and watch the drama unfold. We're old enough to understand what our parents are putting each other through. So we try to make peace. But trying to make things better only escalates the war. Each parent claims we're taking the other parent's side.

We're too old for custody decisions, which most people assume makes the process easier on us. But in actuality, adult kids without such clearly defined boundaries must negotiate separate relationships with each parent, which makes it harder. Parents compete for our affection and our time. Adult children have to figure out whether Mom is going to flip if we spend an afternoon with Dad or whether Dad will think spending Thanksgiving with Mom means we're taking her side. Often, we realize that we were closer to one parent and didn't interact much with the other. "After the divorce, I thought, 'Oh crap. Now I have to deal directly with Dad,'" says one thirty-one-year-old woman.

The Loss of "Home"

Parents start new lives. They remarry, have additional children. Reminiscing about our childhoods becomes off-limits. Bringing up the past only hurts. Some parents don't want us to acknowledge their former spouse in front of them. Parts of our childhoods must be forgotten so our parents can start fresh.

Researchers say those in their early to midtwenties . . . have an especially difficult time. The security of our childhood homes, with all of the images and smells we imagine there, vanishes. "Home is the place where," as Robert Frost famously said, "when you have to go there,/ They have to take you in." The loss of "home" makes adult children feel unrooted, as if the foundation upon which we built our lives were crumbling. Many of us grow unsettled. Our futures suddenly seem unclear. Coming of age is disrupted. One psychologist interviewed said that young adults who have led an uneventful middle-class existence might take parental divorce particularly hard. "It could be the most traumatic thing to happen to you," he said. . . .

Staying Together for the Kids

I used to believe I came from the perfect family. I grew up playing at the beach on Long Island Sound. I collected rocks. My parents read me a story each night and tucked me in. Dad whistled when I curtsied at ballet recitals. Mom beamed. We took Sunday drives, and sometimes we stopped for lunch at clam bars.

But my childhood had a dark side. Dad sometimes drank. Mom and Dad fought so much that Dad packed—and ultimately unpacked—his bags more than once. Mom struggled to make ends meet if Dad's painting business slowed in winter. One night, Dad got so mad at Mom, he punched a hole in a bedroom ceiling. Another time, I listened to Mom bang her fists against Dad's chest. It felt as if the world were collapsing in on me then, too. I'd duck my head under the water in the bathtub, take a walk to the beach, put headphones on and blast music into my ears.

My parents stayed together "for the kids." Fearing we'd never bounce back from their breakup, they waited until my sisters and I were grown to separate. They fell victim to the twenty-five-year itch, like every other couple who bides their time together, slogging through years of marital discontent out of fear that parting ways would do irreversible damage to their children. They wait for the youngest to leave home. Then they duck out and call the kids: "Your father and I haven't been happy for a long time." We're children of the empty nest, only after our parents divorce, we're left with no nest at all.

The Twenty-Five-Year Itch

Most divorces occur after the first seven years of marriage. But the twenty-five-year itch is a growing trend among baby boomers. Rutgers University's National Marriage Project (NMP) says the growth of divorce in this age group has become an accepted fact. According to the National Center for Health Statistics, about 20 percent of today's divorces take place among individuals married more than fifteen years, and of all couples who divorced in 1989 and 1990, the last year recorded, 47 percent had children over the age of eighteen or no children at all. The percentage of Americans sixty-five or older who were divorced or separated jumped 34 percent from 1990 to 2000, says the U.S. Census Bureau. Older couples are splitting up at such high rates, the American Association of Retired Persons (AARP) commissioned a study of midlife divorce in 2004, tracking habits of men and women who divorced in their forties, fifties, or sixties. One surprise: researchers found that 66 percent of these divorces were initiated by women. Our mothers are opting out.

Divorce is increasing among older adults for myriad reasons. For one, boomers married young, and over time, they grew apart. Their ideas about divorce evolved, too. When our parents were children, divorce was considered taboo. These days, splitting up is an accepted fact of life.

Popular culture would like us to believe that separating is the easiest road to self-reinvention. I recently saw an advertisement in *New York* magazine that exemplifies this. A pretty blond woman in her late forties is sitting on a fluffy chair with her legs draped over the armrest and her dogs curled up next to her. She is smiling brightly. The ad reads: *He left me. Good riddance. He never picked up his socks. He thought I was his mother. He didn't make me laugh anymore. He's gone. Who cares? . . . All I wanted was the sofa and the dogs.* Divorce is a time to get what you want. Says feminist writer bell hooks in her 2003 book *Communion,* "Now mid-life and thereafter has become not only a time to reclaim power but also a time to know real love at last."

Cultural views of marriage have shifted, too. Baby boomers, who grew up believing that legal unions should be centered around family, are latching onto the definition of marriage with which younger generations were raised. When younger people marry, we aren't looking only to build a solid family. We're looking for someone to fill our emotional needs, says the National Marriage Project [NMP]. If we don't feel as though our marriages are a spiritualized union of souls, says one 2001 NMP report, we look for a new partner who fills that role, regardless of our kids' ages. In other words, we want to feel butterflies. We're not marrying for practical reasons anymore. When Mom and Dad split up late in life, they're making the same choice. Forget discussing the more traditional reasons for staying together. They want to feel butterflies, too.

Most important, people are living longer. On average, men can expect to make it to their seventy-fifth year and women, their eightieth. Viagra reinvigorated their sex lives. If our parents are in their fifties, they have plenty of time to redefine themselves, including finding a new partner with whom to experience life. Books such as Abigail Trafford's *My Time* and Ken Dychtwald's *The Power Years* have helped define this indulgent second phase of life. Both inspire the boomer set to live as if they were immortal. *Don't simply wait for the grandchildren! Volunteer. Travel. Separate. . . .*

Our Needs Have Been Ignored

We are the lost-nest generation: adult kids who age out of the house only to see our parents decide they've grown apart. Childhood homes are sold in the divorce. We go home to new places where we cannot find the silverware. Our nests are dismantled, blown apart by an unexpected gale.

Hints of the lost nest are evident in popular media. In 2003's *Something's Gotta Give*, starring Jack Nicholson and Diane Keaton, Keaton's adult daughter is shown crying about her parents' divorce just as she's about to run an estate sale at a large auction house. One episode of [MTV's] *The Real World: New York* focuses on a young man who finds out his parents are splitting up during the show. Books such as Joanna Trollope's *Marrying the Mistress* and Helen Fielding's *Bridget Jones's Diary* showcase older adult characters dealing with their divorcing parents.

But the grief of the adult child remains unappreciated and misunderstood. Marriage and family therapists, many of whom have seen an increase of lost-nesters in their waiting rooms, describe only the surface of our pain. Of the numerous articles written on late-life divorce, few reflect on the grown children at the heart of almost every dissolved marriage. It is as though the trend toward late-life marital dissolution comes without consequence.

Researchers have largely ignored us. Only a handful of studies have been conducted on the topic of adult kids of late-life divorce, and nearly all their findings have been incorporated into this book. "For so long, I was the *only* one looking into this," says Teresa Cooney, a family sociologist at the University of Missouri. She authored most of the research on the impact of recent divorce on adult kids in the early to mid-1990s. But funding dried up, and so did Cooney's interest. Only a handful of studies have been done since. Cooney says her work is suddenly getting more attention. There is growing interest in understanding the struggle of the adult child. No doubt this is perpetuated by the increasing number of parents splitting late in life. . . .

Why Divorce Was Not the Answer to a Failing Marriage

Judy Bodmer

In the selection that follows, Judy Bodmer reflects on her experience with a rocky marriage that had progressed from bad to worse. After ten years of marriage, she felt that she had no choice but to divorce her husband. In her mind, the love between them had died, and all that remained was anger and resentment. Following serious reflection about the costs of divorce, she realized that it was not the answer she was seeking. Instead, she renewed her interest in her own life by quitting her job to spend more time with her children and interacting with others outside the home. In addition, she focused on her husband's positive attributes, and he started spending more time with her. Over time, their marriage grew stronger and the love between them was rekindled. Now she is grateful for the time and energy she devoted to putting her marriage back on track. Bodmer is the author of several articles and books, including When Love Dies: How to Save a Hopeless Marriage.

I lay in bed staring at the darkness. My husband, Larry, was snoring softly beside me. We'd just had another fight. I could hardly remember what had started it, but I knew we'd both said ugly, hateful things. Nothing had been resolved. We'd just gotten tired. Now he slept and I lay here, feeling utterly alone.

I crawled out of bed to check on our two sons. David, such a handful while awake, looked like an angel even though his face was sticky from the ice cream he'd eaten earlier. I pulled Matthew's covers back on his small body and smoothed

Judy Bodmer, "My Loveless Marriage: Why Divorce Wasn't the Answer to My Emptiness," *Today's Christian Woman*, vol. 28, no. 1, January–February 2006. Reproduced by permission of the author.

his blond head. He needed a haircut. Working full-time, with two small sons to referee and a house to keep clean, I never had enough time to do it all.

Something drew me to the window. I could see the lights from downtown Seattle. So many people. What were they doing? Were they as lonely as I was? Was there anyone out there who cared? God, I cried, help me find the strength to leave.

Hitting the Wall

After ten years of marriage, I wanted out. Our love hadn't died in the heat of this battle or any other battle. It had died at the bottom of a wall it couldn't climb.

I remember clearly the day I laid the first brick. We'd been married nine months. We went to a movie and I waited for Larry to reach over and take my hand, thus proving the magic was still there. But he didn't and, as the movie progressed, I grew hurt and angry. He shrugged it off, surprised I was upset over such a little thing. To him it was nothing; to me it was the first sign our love wasn't perfect.

As the years passed, I added more bricks. When we were first married, he called me every day from work. But slowly those phone calls grew further apart and finally stopped. When I brought it up, he started calling again, but it wasn't the same. When we watched TV in the evening, he'd fall asleep. When we went out for dinner, he couldn't think of anything to say. His days off were measured by how much he got done—chores, work, and the children took priority. I got the crumbs, and I was starving.

I felt guilty for feeling the way I did; he wasn't abusive, he didn't run around with other women, he didn't drink or do drugs. He came home every night and worked hard to support our family. Despite this, the wall grew, built with bricks of buried anger, unmet needs, silences, and cold shoulders. The marriage books we read made things worse; counseling confused the issues.

Divorce seemed like the only answer. It would give me a chance to start over and find the right person. Yes, it would be hard on the children, but when I was finally happy, I'd be a better parent. In the long run, it would be better for all of us.

Divorce's Price Tag

Before taking that big step, I asked myself some key questions. First, would a divorce make me happier? Somewhere I read that people who divorce tend to remarry the same kind of person, that the root of unhappiness isn't in the people we marry but in ourselves. When I looked at my husband, I knew this was true. The trait in Larry that drew me to him—his calm exterior—also drove me crazy. He never complained, criticized, or caused a fuss. The downside was that when situations arose when he should get angry, he didn't. Once he was cheated in a business deal. I wanted him to confront the man who'd lied to him, but he wouldn't. His love of peace kept him from standing up for himself, making me think he was a moral marshmallow. But if I divorced Larry, I knew I'd marry someone with his same peaceful demeanor. And if I did, my problems would be multiplied by his kids, my kids, child support, and custody battles.

I took a long, hard look at the single mothers I knew. They were exhausted and lonely. There was no one to help soothe crying babies, entertain toddlers, shuttle kids to practices, or help with the house, yard, and car.

Could I afford a divorce financially? The average divorce, according to my paralegal friend, costs about $12,000. My salary was good, but when I looked at our household expenses, there would be hardly enough money to live on, let alone extra money to pay lawyers.

Would my children really be better off in the long run? I looked at the children of my friends who'd divorced. Many of these kids started getting into trouble: staying out all night, drinking, doing drugs, and running away. Most of them were angry and blamed themselves for their parents' split. They took it out on their mother. The father became the hero because he wasn't doing the disciplining. Instead, he brought presents, bought a hot car, and took them fun places the mother couldn't afford. Studies show that even 25 years after a split, children can still have significant emotional problems stemming from their parents' divorce.

What about my friends? I assumed they'd be there for me, but was I being realistic? Four of my friends divorced in one year—I didn't see any of them now. Two of them disappeared, one began leading a lifestyle I couldn't support, and another dated men I didn't care for. Even with the best of intentions, if I divorced, I'd probably lose many, if not all, of my friends.

God showed me I might escape my current pain, but in the long run, divorce extracted a high price. One I wasn't willing to pay.

Fanning the Flames

But I refused to settle for the status quo. From experience, I knew I couldn't change my husband. There was only one person I could change: me. Jesus said, "You hypocrite, first take the plank out of your own eye, and then you will see clearly to remove the speck from your brother's eye" (Matthew 7:5). I got involved in a women's Bible study and started applying what I learned. Before I read a passage, I asked God to examine me. After many sessions on my face before him, honestly asking for forgiveness, I started to change. I became less critical and more forgiving. I stopped taking everything Larry said and did so personally.

I tried new things—taking a writing class, asking a new friend to lunch, volunteering at school. With Larry's blessing, I quit my job to stay home with our children, even though it meant cutting our income in half.

From 1 Corinthians 13, I discovered love isn't a feeling but an action. I decided to treat Larry with love, even though I didn't feel like it. Instead of pointing out his shortcomings, I told him the things he did right. Instead of reading books to see what Larry should be doing differently, I read to discover how I could be a better wife, mother, and friend.

My change in attitude had an amazing effect on Larry. He began spending more time with me. When I stopped overreacting to his comments, he felt freer to share more with me.

My decision to stay went against everything the world told me. Jesus promised, "I have come that [you] may have life and have it to the full" (John 10:10). I decided if God was my God, then I could trust this promise. I asked him to restore my love.

Rekindled

The love I thought had died didn't return in a week, a month, or even in a year. There were times I wanted to give up. But I clung to God's promise that he would give me the desire of my heart.

One weekend Larry and I went away. Before we left, we prayed and drew a line in the sand. Everything that had happened before was over; this was a new beginning. That weekend I experienced a new passion for my husband. The flame I thought was dead was rekindled.

Today when I sit in church worshiping God, I shudder at what I almost threw away. Larry and I laugh over things that used to drive me nuts, like his falling asleep in front of the TV. I can tell Larry anything, and he listens. Just yesterday he sent me a fax just to tell me he loves me.

At night when we lay curled up together, I reach over and touch him just to reassure myself he's still there. The love I have is strong. It's born out of suffering and obedience. The pain, tears, and struggles to get to this point were worth it for these rich rewards. There is hope for loveless marriages. Our relationship is living proof.

Learning Valuable Lessons from Divorce

Hugo Schwyzer

Being married and divorced more than once is not that uncommon in contemporary America. Once shunned by fellow citizens, most divorced men and women no longer fear societal ramifications for their actions and move on to form other relationships. In the following selection, Hugh Schwyzer discusses his three previous divorces and an upcoming marriage. He has come to realize that his past marriages have helped him become a better person. Ultimately, without going through three divorces, he believes, he would not have acquired the relationship skills he now possesses. He also feels more confident about marital expectations and realities. Schwyzer is a history professor at Pasadena Community College in California.

As our wedding date draws closer and the anticipation grows, I've also been thinking—just a little bit—about divorce. No, I'm happy to say that I'm not filled with foreboding. My certainty about the woman who will be my wife is deep, far deeper than I've known with anyone else! I feel blessed that my fiancee is willing to marry a man who does have a track record of three divorces; her faith in me and our mutual belief that the past is not necessarily the best predictor of future behavior are great reassurances.

Lessons Learned

But this week, I've been filled with a strange sense of gratitude for my three previous marriages. I'm keenly aware of the fact that I learned a great deal in each of them, and though all of the lessons were painful, they were ultimately very positive in my life. Indeed, as far as I can tell, I cannot imagine having the relationship skills I do possess if I hadn't gone through each of these brief, difficult, but nonetheless significant marriages. If nothing else, my past has taught me a great deal about what *not* to do in a new marriage; it has also liberated me from most of the unhelpful fantasies about what relationships are.

I know I'm treading dangerously close to the logical fallacy of *post hoc ergo propter hoc* ("after this, therefore on account of this.") Obviously, lots and lots of men have become wonderful, thoughtful husbands and fathers without having multiple prior marriages! And let me hasten to argue that I don't think that divorce is an inherently good thing. But I also have learned that "failed marriages" can have a profoundly positive effect upon those who survive them, provided those who came out of that marriage chose to learn the lessons offered by the experience. And I think it's safe to say that for some of us, we might never have learned our lessons in any other way.

I don't write in any detail about my previous marriages. All were brief; none lasted longer than a few years. All ended for different reasons, and they ended in different ways. While my second marriage ended stormily and abruptly, my third marriage ended very gently and thoughtfully. With this final divorce, my ex-wife and I spent a great deal of time in therapy, and as a result of that process came to see our entire marriage in a different light.

Our marriage counselor was—and is—a prominent Christian psychologist. He was one of the early graduates of Fuller Seminary's Graduate School of Psychology. Obviously, I expected "Dr. K." to take a strongly anti-divorce tack. But he surprised us, especially one day when my former wife, crying in his office, said "Divorce makes me feel like such a failure." Dr. K said something remarkable (I paraphrase, though I remember it vividly): "You know, I used to think divorce was always a sign of failure. But I don't use the term 'failed marriage' as lightly any more. I think the best divorces are more like graduations—they mark the moment when the marriage has served its purpose, both spouses have learned all that they could from it, and it's time for them to move on." . . .

Coming from the mouth of a famous Fuller Ph.D whom I knew came from a conservative Dutch Calvinist background, this was pretty stunning! (And for those of you who know the small Pasadena community of "Fuller folk", don't try and guess the identity of Dr. K.) But as shocking as it was, it rang true. These were not easy words offered to comfort two guilt-ridden people. Dr. K was drawing attention to the very real possibility that in some instances, divorce can (for all its attendant hurts and disappointments) be a profoundly positive experience, particularly when it occurs in a kind, civil atmosphere where each partner gets a chance to share their personal pain and grief.

Divorce Can Be Forgiven

My evangelical theology and my romantic fantasy both tell me the same thing: all marriages should last forever. It's hard to extricate oneself from that belief, and even now, I'm not entirely convinced that we ought to try and do so. There's certainly some very real value in making a lifelong commitment, even if one's own "growth trajectory" makes it impossible to continue to honor that commitment after a certain period of time. At the same time, there's no point in having divorced folks wander around guilt-ridden. I can't tell you how many of my Christian friends who are in their second or third marriages still feel shame and guilt about their divorces. For those of us who believe in forgiveness, and who belong to religious communities that honor the possibility of remarriage after divorce, such guilt seems almost prideful. If regeneration is a process that can happen over and over again, as our faith tells us is possible, then surely we are defying God's grace if we continue to beat ourselves up for past marriages that were ended by dissolution rather than death!

But I don't just believe that divorce is an "evil" that can be forgiven. Though many divorces are bitter and nasty, not all of them need be. I've gone the bitter and angry route (in my second), and I've gone the loving, charitable, and (dare I say it) "positive" route (in my third.) Thus in my own experience, I have witnessed the very real redemptive possibilities that can be found in the experience of marital dissolution.

In this last divorce process, which lasted months, I allowed myself to experience the unique "refining fire" that the end-of-marriage process can offer. I am absolutely convinced that few other experiences, if any, can force one to confront the realities of one's own sinfulness and one's own selfishness! In that marriage, especially in the drawn-out process which ended it, I faced some colossally uncomfortable truths about myself. In the safe atmosphere of the therapist's office, my ex-wife and I confronted each other. But rather than just "dump", we both took the time to hear what we were being told. And by doing that "hearing work", we not only validated the other's experience, we came to terms with facts about ourselves we would never otherwise have seen.

Towards a Healthy Marriage

Strange thing: We began the therapy process with Dr. K hoping the marriage could be saved. But we continued to see him for weeks *after* we had both agreed to divorce. Our goal in those remaining sessions was not to find a way to stay together; rather, it was to make the separation experience as vital, as cleansing, and as cathartic as possible. It was a great gift that my ex-wife and I gave each other. On the final night of therapy, I walked my ex to her car after we were finished. "I feel elated", she said, "giddy." "I know", I replied, "me too." We hugged tightly for what would be the last time, and just before saying goodbye, we thanked each other once again. The thank you was for all the effort each had put into the marriage, but also all the honesty and forgiveness and grace we had each brought to the divorce experience. I wept as I drove away that night, but I was not in agony; the tears were tears of incredible gratitude for the amazing experience that I had just completed.

Of course, saying that there is such a thing as a "good divorce" or that it can be like "graduation" is not the same thing as saying that divorce is the best possible outcome! Obviously, in the best and healthiest marriages, that experience of being in the "crucible", with all one's selfish impurities melting away, will happen within the relationship itself, and not only in the therapist's office as one prepares for the final goodbye! As I prepare to get married again, I am filled with genuine confidence that my beloved and I will be able to challenge each other and help each other transform—all while making the marriage grow and survive.

I am confident of this not only because of the tremendous depth of love I have for my fiancee, but because I feel that we each have a formidable "skill set" of spiritual and psychological tools that we can bring to the table. In my case, I acquired those tools from many sources: from various spiritual communities, wise mentors and pastors, dear friends, and the grace of a loving God. But I also acquired those tools through the immensely painful—and yet also immensely transformative—experience of my three divorces. When I stand with my bride-to-be not long from now, I will have thoughts of no one but her in my head. She is my "now", and she is my "tomorrow", and Lord willing, will be my tomorrow for all the tomorrows to come. But I am only truly ready to be hers because of all of my yesterdays, and all that they taught me.

A Woman and Her
Ex-husband Create a Loving
Family for Their Sons

Laura Stavoe

One of the biggest concerns for researchers and parents alike is how to help children adjust after a divorce. All agree that it is important to provide children with a stable home environment and the assurance that they are loved by both parents. In the following selection, Laura Stavoe describes the way she and her ex-husband were able to help their twin sons overcome their feelings of loss and abandonment following their divorce. At first, the children responded with fear and sadness, but as Stavoe and her ex-husband worked together to provide them with two equally loving homes just a mile from each other, their fears were allayed. Stavoe and her ex-husband found ways of dealing with the children in a loving way after learning to be unselfish and caring with each other. Now, the two boys happily spend equal time with both parents in stable households. Stavoe is a freelance writer whose articles have appeared in Ladies' Home Journal, Parenting, *and* American Baby.

G reg invites me into his new house. The carpet is white, spotless—clearly, the former owner didn't have twins.

Our 5-year-old boys run to greet me and give me a tour. Other than the carpet and equally clean appliances, the house looks a lot like mine. It's a small three-bedroom with an attached garage—in the subdivision next to the one my house is in, the house Greg and I bought together seven years ago.

Gabe and Dylan point out their new plaid sheets, then run to show off the rest of the house, still full of unpacked boxes.

For years I refused to consider divorce, or even separation, mainly because I didn't want my children to have to shuffle between houses. I wanted them to know where home was— one address, one phone number, one master bedroom where they could find two parents any time of night. So even after our marriage crumbled, I clung to the hope that by some miracle, things would work out.

Pains of Separation

Finally, there came an August evening when we had to tell our 4-year-olds that Mom and Dad were going to live in separate houses.

Gabe yelled "No!" over and over. He made sure that one part of his body was touching each of us as he sobbed, his head on my lap, his ankles hooked onto his dad's legs.

Dylan said nothing and went into the backyard to play with his toy golf set. It wasn't until late that night that he looked up at me and said, "But now we won't have a dad."

"Daddy will always be your dad," I told him, but I couldn't deny that all our relationships were changing.

Greg moved out to his folks' place, and I marked calendars with M's and D's to remind the boys and me which house they would go to after school and whether it would be for dinner or overnight. I hated the calendars. They represented instability. They reminded me of our failure.

Dylan grins as he takes me to see the dining area that looks out onto the patio. I recognize the palm plant that used to sit in our living room.

"We have four chairs," he tells me. "Someday you can eat dinner here." It's true. I might. Not everything has turned out as I feared.

An Unselfish Act

Greg and I spent too much time in lawyers' offices the past year, dividing up bank accounts and summer vacations. We spent more than an hour just on Christmas, trying to find time for the kids with my family in Chicago and Greg's in Boise. The discussion disintegrated into a fight the same way most had at home or in front of marriage counselors. We both felt hurt, scared, angry, and misunderstood.

The mediator suggested we decide holidays later, so we rode down the elevator together in silence. I felt fed up with both of us. How were we ever going to do right by our sons?

That night, Greg called. "The boys love being with your folks and all of their cousins," he said. "I think they should go with you."

I don't know which was more remarkable, Greg's selflessness or the fact that I noticed it. I knew how difficult it was for him to offer to spend Christmas away from his sons. I was reminded of how much he loves them, how committed to them he's always been. And something began to change: I started to trust Greg in a different way, to recognize that when it came to our children, his intentions were always good.

Over the past year, each of us has watched the other make many similar decisions. Some were big, like agreeing to live near each other, and others small, like changing nights for dinner. And each time, the trust between us has grown.

By the time the legal documents deemed the marriage officially over, I'd come to see that a part of our relationship lives on in our sons and in our mutual love for them. Gabe knows he always has access to both parents. And Dylan never questions whether he has a dad.

Making It Work

When the tour is over, the boys run out to my car in their pajamas, hair smelling of an unfamiliar brand of shampoo. Greg kisses them, tells me to drive carefully on the "long" trip home. We both smile at this.

On the way, Gabe and Dylan chatter about the house, the fireplace, the cool workroom where their dad will build them furniture. Then their other house comes into view, the one with more established foliage (and carpet stains). They climb out of the car and run to play at the basketball hoop they received for their fifth birthday. I realize that they see their homes in terms of what each has to offer. One is on a cul-de-sac; the other has a jungle gym. Both have what the boys need: safety, warmth, love.

I have learned that there's a more important question than one house or two, and that is: What is life like in those houses? Our sons have learned that they can find home in two places.

A Woman's Marital Views Are Shaped by Her Parents' Divorce

Amy Conway

In the following selection, Amy Conway writes about her experiences before, during, and after her parents' divorce. Up until the age of thirteen, she and her brother had lived what she thought was an idyllic, middle-class life. But the day her parents told her that they were getting a divorce made her realize that there must have been problems in her family all along. Looking back, she realizes that her mother and father were two very different people who probably never should have gotten married in the first place. Although her parents' divorce was fairly amicable, her relationship with both of her them changed. Now, many years later, Conway is in her own marriage and is expecting a child. She is determined to make sure that her child has a safe and stable home life like the one her husband experienced. Conway is a writer who lives in New York City.

Everything changed in an afternoon. When I was thirteen, my parents gathered my brother and me into the kitchen after school to tell us that our father would be moving out. I'd had no idea that their marriage wouldn't last forever—but then again, neither had my mother until a few weeks earlier, when she discovered my father whispering to his girlfriend on the phone in the middle of the night.

Twenty years, three stepparents, and countless crying jags later, the story has no ending. I adapted, just as they say kids do. But divorce is more than a crisis to be worked through. No matter how well I weathered the storm when it was at its worst, I still emerged dripping with its effects, and feel a bit waterlogged to this day. Old doubts and questions linger, and mingle with fresh ones that arise as my parents and I get on with our lives. Married myself and seven months pregnant as I write this, I now fervently hope that my husband and I can give our children a life so solid they won't even think to question its foundation, like the one I knew until that afternoon.

The Perfect Life

My older brother, Andrew, and I were raised in a suburb of St. Louis where the leafy streets, old brick houses, and diverse, liberal community attracted academic families like ours. We played hide-and-seek after dinner with the neighborhood kids while the moms chatted on the front porches. We piled into the car for long trips to Maine or Florida in the summer. We read lots of books, watched too much television, and got "Excellents" on our report cards. It was a model 1970s middle-class upbringing, an utterly carefree existence. Only occasionally did we get glimpses of how lucky we were, when we saw that our Christmas tree had a few more presents beneath it, that some fathers bellowed at their children, that a few of our friends wore keys around their necks to let themselves in after school. But mostly, we took our happiness for granted, because we were fortunate enough to be unaware that anything else was a possibility.

Andrew and I weren't the only ones who assumed that our life would go on that way. When my parents separated, other families were shocked, and questioned their own stability; kids said to their parents, "If Amy and Andrew's mom and dad are getting divorced, are you going to, too?" There hadn't been a moment of tension or discord in our house. My parents never fought. Later, I realized that I also never saw them hug or kiss or hold hands.

The Beginning of the End

I would learn that while my parents worked well together as mom and dad, they weren't so good at being husband and wife. They had been high school sweethearts and continued dating while my father went to Princeton to study philosophy. After graduation in 1960, they got married, for less than romantic reasons: after so many years together, it just seemed like the next step, especially since it meant my father could pursue his Ph.D. without accepting more money from his own father. So, like many women of her generation, my mother worked, as a secretary, to support them while he continued his education and pursued his career.

They were just two young people doing what they thought they should be doing with their lives, not analyzing every move and mood as today's hyperaware twenty-somethings do. But it soon became clear that their divergent personalities—she is outgoing, social, and emotional, while he is quiet, wry, and intellectual—did not make for a perfect fit. He wasn't satisfied, and she felt inadequate, burdened with the responsibility to become the wife he wanted, someone more bookish and academic. Many years later, he told her that if he could have snapped his fingers to undo their marriage in those early days, he would have. Of course, it would have taken more than a magic spell or a wish, but he could have left then, before they had children, with much less trouble and heartache than at any other moment later in their relationship. . . .

The fact that they had little in common aside from their love for us was disguised for years by the rhythm of everyday family life. Our house was a cheerful place, with the doors always open for neighbors to come on in, a cat and dog underfoot, and all four of us home for dinner. It didn't seem odd that my parents didn't spend much time together alone, rarely went out to eat or to the movies. My mother's friends were the women down the street, my father's were the professors in his department, and with their extended families across the country, there were few people they socialized with together. I can recall having a babysitter only about three or four times in my life—our parents were simply always home. They nurtured us, not their relationship.

This version of family suited my mother just fine. My father, however, still wanted more. He found it in a colleague, a cerebral woman several years younger, never married and without children. I don't know whether or not he planned to leave my mother for her, whether or not he would ever have summoned the nerve. I expect my mother did him a favor by discovering their affair. She did his dirty work for him.

He seized the opportunity, though, telling my mother that he hadn't been happy in years, that he wanted a separation. After a few weeks of tears and trips to a marriage counselor, my mother gradually began to realize that he meant it. Even so, she hoped she was just calling his bluff when she told him that it was time to speak to Andrew and me; she thought the prospect of facing us would make him change his mind. It didn't. So there we were, perched on bar stools in the kitchen as my mother said that they had something to tell us, something very sad. I could see how nervous she was, which scared me. But she managed not to cry as she said that my father would be moving out. My dad's voice broke as he quietly backed her up, assuring us that they both loved us as much as ever. Andrew acted nonplussed, and would soon head off to a friend's house. I burst into inappropriate laughter, out of fear or panic. . . .

A Year of Transition

During those first few months my mother was out of her mind. She gathered together all the letters my father had ever written her and dumped them in a heap behind his new apartment. If both his and his girlfriend's phones were busy, she would have operators make emergency interrupts, over and over and over again. But of all the emotions she felt, she was not depressed. She realized that she had been depressed for years, and now that feeling was replaced by sheer terror. My father had taken care of the house and all the bills—she didn't even know who held their mortgage. She was also struggling financially. My dad paid child support and helped with other expenses, but there just wasn't much money to go around, with their salaries (she had started working full-time as a secretary several years earlier) now paying for two households. She took a second job as a salesperson in the hosiery department of a local department store a few nights a week. She hated it, and came home worn out from dealing with the customers like the woman who tried to return pantyhose stained with menstrual blood, claiming they'd never been worn. My mom didn't argue with her. She just wanted to make some money and get back to Andrew and me.

She did her best not to show us how out of control she felt. And in general, our parents tried to do everything right. They assured Andrew and me that the separation had nothing to do with us, didn't badmouth each other, and had me see a child psychologist. Talking to someone impartial helped me identify my fears and feelings, and I enjoyed the notoriety of being picked up after school to go to the shrink. (My brother, just starting his senior year of high school, refused to see the psychologist, and in general played the part of aloof teenager.) My father moved into a small apartment across town—the girlfriend was on sabbatical in another state, so we didn't have her to worry about right away—and we set up a visitation schedule. Andrew and I would see our dad on Tuesday and Thursday nights. Andrew often skipped it in favor of band practice, but my dad would pick me up, take me to Steak & Shake or to his apartment where we would make dinner. I would do some homework, we would watch TV, and he'd drop me off back at home a few hours later.

It was just assumed that we would live, seven nights a week, with our mom, in our house. Perhaps my father didn't want to disrupt her life any more than he already had, or maybe one or both of them realized that he wouldn't know what to do with us on his own (in fact, my mother recalls that Tuesdays and Thursdays were chosen in part because they were "good TV nights"). But the arrangement took away the thing my father was best at: just being there. With no overnight visits, there wasn't a room for me at his apartment. Gone were the familiarity, the routine, the security. Instead we had dates, with chats about things that didn't help us get to know each other better, but just showed how much was missing.

It was a strange transitional year, as we picked our way through the remains of our broken family. The following fall, Andrew went away to college, I began high school, my mother adjusted to being a single mom, and my dad started living with his girlfriend. We were moving on, each of us on our own. . . .

Lessons Learned

Though our relationships with our parents haven't changed drastically since we were adolescents, much else has. Our mother has remarried and divorced, and is more content today, single, than she was with either husband. Our father is still searching. He left his second wife for a third several years ago, and divorced again recently. The experiences of watching my mother and father go through the messy machinations of dating, attending their weddings, and being saddled with stepparents and stepsiblings have ranged from mildly unpleasant to traumatic, though I don't think such events have to be upsetting. If either of my parents had made solid matches, exploring new relationships could have been wonderful.

In my own romantic life, I've had one serious, long-term boyfriend after the other since that first love in high school, but I wasn't always faithful. Whether this was because of what I saw in my own family growing up or simply youthful indiscretion, I don't know. Meeting the right person could be what broke the pattern. When I was in my mid-twenties and had recently moved to New York, I met the man who would become my husband, a remarkably solid and secure person (with married parents), and was soon thinking about the future. Marriage didn't scare me, perhaps because I remember my own early childhood as being so happy. And I can see how different my marriage is from my parents'; it's a true, honest partnership. But there are still echoes from the divorce. The idea of my father telling my mother, too late, that he had been miserable for years haunts me. I have rather irrationally made my husband promise to alert me immediately if he feels an inkling of dissatisfaction with me—if I'm not smart enough, too smart, too fat, too thin, too short, too tall—so I have the chance to change.

My husband and I already feel like a family, just the two of us. When our child arrives, we both want to provide the same thing for this vulnerable little person: a loving, stable place that insulates against the rest of the world. The only difference is that in matters of family, my husband has the confidence, or perhaps naivete, that comes from being brought up in a home without divorce—the belief that once married, you stay married. I know better. I just have hope.

The Importance of Same-Sex Civil Union Divorces

Kathy Anderson

As more states pass legislation allowing same-sex couples to enter into civil unions, the divorce rate among homosexual couples will rise as well. In the following selection, Kathy Anderson describes the break up of her civil union granted in Vermont. Although she and her partner were together for over five years, their civil union lasted only fourteen months. Given that few states recognize same-sex civil unions, it was difficult for her to obtain a divorce in her home state of New Jersey. Vermont, in fact, requires that one of the partners become a Vermont resident for one year before a divorce can be obtained. In most states, legal dissolution of a same-sex civil union is nearly impossible. Anderson asserts that it is important to her and to other same-sex couples to obtain a divorce decree because doing so not only ensures that the civil union has ended and assets can be divided equitably, but it also recognizes that a real relationship existed in the first place. Anderson is a freelance writer whose work has appeared in a number of anthologies. She is also a member of the New Jersey Library Association's Lesbian and Gay Round Table.

The moment of the Big Kaboom, when I knew our relationship was over just 14 months after our Vermont civil union, I knew instinctively that I would not be attending the lesbian support group at the gay and lesbian community center for help. Suddenly I had more in common with the straight married neighbors in our New Jersey town.

In August 2002 my partner and I had gone to City Hall in Burlington, Vt., and filled out applications for a civil union license. We pledged traditional vows before a justice of the peace on the banks of Lake Champlain. At our wedding reception in New Jersey a few months later, our friends and family toasted us and danced to a live band.

This was no lesbian second date, no "pull up the U-Haul." After five years together we had carefully prepared for commitment. We had pre-marriage counseling with our Dignity USA chapter priest. We created wills and powers of attorney. Still, nothing prepared me for what the radical act of marriage felt like; for the wild immensity of the ritual: for how deeply open I felt to the sky, the lake, our future together—how connected I felt to our families in spirit.

The Need for a Divorce

Longtime residents of New Jersey, we had chosen a civil union in Vermont as the most legal way to marry at the time, announcing it to loved ones with engraved invitations. So when the Big Kaboom hit, there was no way to minimize it to myself or others, no way to slink away and then months later tell all those people, "Oh, yeah, we broke up."

This was no breakup. This was a divorce.

This was a 10-page separation agreement. This was a docket number on a legal complaint for dissolution. This was me swearing to a judge that I told the truth.

Why bother getting a legal dissolution? After all, it's a tremendous challenge. While Vermont has no residency requirement for getting a civil union, for dissolution it has a one-year residency requirement for at least one party. Couples who are joined in Vermont and later ask their state courts to dissolve their out-of-state union face an uphill battle.

People have asked me kindly, "How legal was it anyway? You live in New Jersey, and your civil union only really counted if you live in Vermont." Talking to a friend, I struggled to put into words why it felt so vital. It wasn't for financial reasons: We had no children, no joint property. "Why, not suing for dissolution would invalidate the whole thing," she said wisely. And that was it, the word I was searching for. I would not invalidate our civil union by agreeing that it didn't count.

Joining a Support Group

Grieving, heartsick, I began dissolution proceedings and joined a women's divorce support group, sponsored by the local chapter of the National Organization for Women, searching for closure and healing. Every week, as new women joined the circle, I had to come out again as a lesbian married in a civil union. When I said my partner was a woman, the only difference I noticed in other women's reactions was a perceptible leaning-in, as if they were hoping for something new, a uniquely lesbian slant on this painful journey—because the tales told around that table were as predictable as nightfall. But there was nothing unique in my story.

Slowly my divorce group buddies and I healed together; learned that forgiveness saves your life; that taking responsibility for your own part, whether big or small, makes you a divorce survivor, not a victim.

I still believe that marriage will bring most of us incredible blessings. But when our marriages don't work, I hope we insist on proper divorces, with lawyers and judges in our courts, because we deserve to honor our unions with this validation too. We deserve help breaking up households and navigating custody of children. Just as we insist on the right to marry, we have to demand that the legal system help us dissolve our unions when we have to. Because these are not empty ceremonial gestures we are making in Vermont and Massachusetts and Oregon and San Francisco. Our marriages count.

Organizations to Contact

**Association for Children for Enforcement
of Support (ACES)**
PO Box 7842, Fredericksburg, VA 22404
(888) 310-2237
e-mail: aces@childsupport-aces.org
Web site: www.childsupport-aces.org

ACES is a nonprofit child-support organization dedicated to assisting disadvantaged children whose parents fail to meet the legal and moral obligations of child support and/or visitation. It is the largest national grassroots child-support advocacy organization in the United States, with forty thousand members and 165 chapters in forty-five states.

**Association of Family and
Conciliation Courts (AFCC)**
6525 Grand Teton Plaza, Madison, WI 53719
(608) 664-3750 • fax: (608) 664-3751
e-mail: afcc@afccnet.org
Web site: www.afccnet.org

Founded in 1963, the AFCC has grown from a handful of California counselors and judges to an international association of judges, lawyers, mediators, custody evaluators, parent educators, court administrators, counselors, researchers, academics, and other professionals dedicated to the resolution of family conflict. Members attempt to find creative solutions to divorce-related issues such as child custody mediation, parenting coordination, and divorce education. In addition to annual conferences, the AFCC regularly publishes a journal, *Family Court Review,* as well as books and pamphlets addressing contemporary issues in the family court system.

Child Welfare League of America (CWLA)
440 First St. NW, 3rd Fl., Washington, DC 20001-2085
(202) 638-2952 • fax: (202) 638-4004
Web site: www.cwla.org

Founded in 1920, the CWLA is the nation's oldest and largest membership-based child welfare organization. Its primary objective is to make children a national priority by providing direct support to agencies that serve children and families. In addition to sponsoring annual conferences and providing consultation services to child welfare agencies, the CWLA regularly publishes many different types of materials concerning child welfare issues, including "CWLA Standards of Excellence for Services to Strengthen and Preserve Families with Children" and the *Child Welfare Journal.*

Children's Rights Council (CRC)
6200 Editors Park Dr., Suite 103, Hyattsville, MD 20782
(301) 559-3120 • fax: (301) 559-3124
e-mail: crcdc@erols.com
Web site: http://gocrc.com

Formed in 1985, the Children's Rights Council is a national nonprofit organization based in Washington, D.C., that works to assure children meaningful and continuing contact with both their parents and extended family regardless of the parents' marital status. The CRC distributes books and pamphlets specializing in shared custody information for children and parents.

Concerned Women for America (CWA)
1015 Fifteenth St. NW, Suite 1100, Washington, DC 20005
(202) 488-7000 • fax: (301) 559-3124
Web site: www.cwfa.org

The CWA is an educational and legal defense foundation that seeks to strengthen the traditional family by employing Christian principles. In addition to providing a collection of the latest research and news concerning the maintenance of the

167

nuclear family, the CWA publishes *Family Voice*, a monthly magazine for members, and offers many brochures and pamphlets including *Why Children Need Fathers: Five Critical Trends*.

Divorce Care

PO Box 1739, Wake Forest, NC 27588
(800) 489-7778
e-mail: info@divorcecare.org
Web site: www.divorcecare.com

Divorce Care is sponsored by Church Initiative, Inc., a nondenominational, nonprofit ministry, providing thousands of churches in the United States, Canada, the United Kingdom, South Africa, Australia, and several other countries with videos and other media that focus on maintaining strong family bonds. Divorce Care groups meet weekly to support members who are going through divorces. The organization also sponsors Divorce Care for Kids, which helps children deal with their parents' divorce.

Family Research Council (FRC)

801 G St. NW, Washington, DC 20001
(202) 393-2100 • fax: (202) 393-2134
Web site: www.frc.org

The FRC supports traditional marriage and family using Judeo-Christian values. It has helped shape public debate and formulated public policy that upholds the institutions of marriage and the family. One such recent political action took the form of a petition to urge U.S. senators to pass a bill to preserve one-man/one-woman marriage. In addition to numerous position papers and research reports, the FRC also publishes two journals, *InFocus* and *Family Policy*.

Kids' Turn

1242 Market St., 2nd Fl., San Francisco, CA 94102-4802
(415) 437-0700

e-mail: kidsturn@earthlink.net
Web site: www.kidsturn.org

Kids' Turn is a private nonprofit organization formed in 1989. It provides educational programs for children, adolescents and parents experiencing separation or divorce. Kids' Turn publishes *Good Parenting Through Your Divorce*, a book based on the materials used in the Kids' Turn programs.

National Association of Child Advocates (NACA)
1522 K St. NW, Suite 600, Washington, DC 20005
(202) 289-0777 • fax: (202) 289-0776

NACA is a network of state and local child-advocacy organizations addressing important issues such as government allocations for children, child health insurance programs, welfare reform, state legislation affecting kids, and leadership training for child advocates. NACA strives to change policy in areas of health care, education, child care, child support, and juvenile justice. Although NACA and its forty-four member organizations do not provide individual services, they can provide information on the most current legislation and policies affecting children and families.

National Fatherhood Initiative (NFI)
101 Lake Forest Blvd., Suite 360, Gaithersburg, MD 20877
(301) 948-0599 • fax: (301) 948-4325
Web site: www.fatherhood.org

The NFI is a nonprofit organization who seeks to improve the well-being of children by increasing the proportion of children growing up with involved, responsible, and committed fathers. Through public awareness campaigns and research, the NFI attempts to educate the public about issues facing fathers and their children. Some of the NFI's most recent publications include *With This Ring . . . A National Survey of Marriage and the Family* and *Family Structure, Father Closeness, and Delinquency.*

National Organization of Single Mothers (NOSM)
PO Box 68, Midland, NC 28107
(704) 888-5437 • fax: (704) 888-1752
e-mail: info@singlemothers.org
Web site: www.singlemothers.org

NOSM is a nonprofit organization dedicated to helping single mothers cope with the challenges of raising children alone. In addition to providing online support groups, the organization also publishes a quarterly magazine, *Single Mother: A Support Group in Your Hand,* and a resource book, *The Complete Single Mother: Reassuring Answers to Your Most Challenging Concerns,* now in its third edition.

Parents Without Partners (PWP)
1650 South Dixie Hwy., Suite 510, Boca Raton, FL 33432
(561) 391-8833 • fax: (561) 395-8557
Web site: www.parentswithoutpartners.org

Founded in 1957, PWP is the largest international nonprofit membership organization devoted to the welfare and interests of single parents and their children. PWP offers an environment for support, friendship, and the exchange of parenting techniques. In addition to maintaining over two hundred chapters in the United States, Canada, and Australia, PWP holds annual international conferences to help keep members up-to-date on issues affecting single parents.

Sandcastles Program
PO Box 402691, Miami Beach, FL 33140
(205) 978-5000 • fax: (205) 978-5005
e-mail: mgary@mgaryneuman.com
Web site: www.mgaryneuman.com/sp.html

The Sandcastles Program is an internationally recognized program designed to help children heal after their parents divorce. It is a three-and-a-half-hour, onetime group session for children of divorce between the ages of six and seventeen. The program was first instituted in Miami-Dade County, Florida,

and is now mandatory there and in over a dozen other juris-
dictions throughout the country. In these counties, no final
divorce decree will be granted any couple whose minor children do not participate in the Sandcastles Program. M. Gary
Neuman, the founder of the Sandcastles Program, is a psycho-
therapist, rabbi, and the author of several books, including
Helping Your Kids Cope with Divorce the Sandcastles Way.

Single Parent Resource Center (SPRC)
31 E. Twenty-eighth St., 2nd Fl., New York, NY 10016
(212) 951-7030
Web site: www.singleparentusa.com

SPRC, an independent nonprofit organization, was founded in
1975 by the Community Service Society of New York to provide services and support for single parents. SPRC sponsors
Single Parent USA, a clearinghouse for information on single-
parent organizations in the United States and around the
world to enable single-parent groups and organizations to
share information on program development, service models,
and techniques and to facilitate referral of single parents to
groups or support programs in their local communities.

Stepfamily Association of America (SAA)
650 J St., Suite 205, Lincoln, NE 68508
(800) 735-0329
e-mail: stepfamfs@aol.com
Web site: www.saafamilies.org

Founded in 1977, SAA is a national nonprofit membership organization dedicated to successful stepfamily living. It provides information, education, support, and advocacy for stepfamilies and those who work with them. In addition to a
quarterly journal, *SAA Families*, the SAA also regularly publishes research and reports, including "Divorce and Remarriage in Later Adulthood."

Bibliography

Books

Constance R. Ahrons — *We're Still Family: What Grown Children Have to Say About Their Parents' Divorce.* New York: HarperCollins, 2004.

Jane Bingham — *Why Do Families Break Up?* Chicago: Raintree, 2005.

Les Carter — *Grace and Divorce: God's Healing Gift to Those Whose Marriages Fall Short.* San Francisco: Jossey-Bass, 2005.

Alison Clarke-Stewart and Cornelia Brentano — *Divorce: Causes and Consequences.* New Haven, CT: Yale University Press, 2006.

Christine A. Coates and E. Robert LaCrosse — *Learning from Divorce: How to Take Responsibility, Stop the Blame, and Move On.* San Francisco: Jossey-Bass, 2003.

Marilyn Coleman and Larry Ganong, eds. — *Points and Counterpoints: Controversial Relationship and Family Issues in the 21st Century.* Los Angeles: Roxbury, 2003.

Shelia Ellison — *The Courage to Love Again: Creating Happy, Healthy Relationships After Divorce.* San Francisco: HarperSanFrancisco, 2002.

Robert E. Emery   *The Truth About Children and Divorce: Groundbreaking Research and Advice for Dealing with the Emotions So You and Your Children Can Thrive.* New York: Viking, 2004.

Grace Gabe and   *Step Wars.* New York: St. Martin's,
Jean   2004.
Lipman-Blumen

John H. Harvey   *Children of Divorce: Stories of Loss and Growth.* Mahwah, NJ: Lawrence Erlbaum Associates, 2004.
and Mark A. Fine

bell hooks   *Communion: The Female Search for Love.* New York: HarperPerennial, 2002.

Richard J. Jenks   *Annulments and the Catholic Church: Healing or Hurtful?* New York: Haworth, 2002.

Barbara LeBey   *Family Estrangements: How They Begin, How to Mend Them, How to Cope with Them.* New York: Bantam, 2001.

Cynthia   *The Divorce Helpbook for Teens.* Atascadero, CA: Impact, 2004.
MacGregor

Perry Netter   *Divorce Is a Mitzvah: A Practical Guide to Find Wholeness and Holiness When Your Marriage Dies.* Woodstock, VT: Jewish Lights, 2002.

Pamela Paul   *The Starter Marriage and the Future of Matrimony.* New York: Villard, 2002.

Laura Petherbridge	*When Your Marriage Dies: Answers to Questions About Separation and Divorce.* Colorado Springs, CO: Life Journey, 2005.
Elizabeth Price	*Divorce and Teens: When a Family Splits Apart.* Berkeley Heights, NJ: Enslow, 2004.
Anne O'Connor	*The Truth About Stepfamilies: Real American Stepfamilies Speak Out.* New York: Marlowe, 2003.
Omid Safi, ed.	*Progressive Muslims: On Justice, Gender, and Pluralism.* Oxford, UK: One World, 2003.
Susan Lee Smith	*Wedding Vows: Beyond Love, Honor, and Cherish.* New York: Warner, 2001.
Abigail Trafford	*My Time: Making the Most of the Rest of Your Life.* New York: Basic Books, 2004.
Peggy Vaughn	*The Monogamy Myth.* 3rd ed. New York: Newmarket, 2003.
Victoria Vondenberger	*Catholics, Marriage and Divorce: Real People, Real Questions.* Cincinnati: St. Anthony Messenger, 2004.

Periodicals

David Adams-Smith	"Survivors: Children Of Divorce," *News Photographer*, February 2006.

Paul R. Amato   "Reconciling Divergent Perspectives: Judith Wallerstein, Quantitative Family Research, and Children of Divorce," *Family Relations*, 2003.

Adele M. Brodkin   "When Parents Separate," *Scholastic Parent & Child*, October 2005.

Jill Brooke   "Personal Style, Unleashed by Divorce," *New York Times*, March 23, 2006.

Allan Carlson   "Broken Homes, and Hearts," *National Review*, November 7, 2005.

Christian Century   "No Good Divorce," February 7, 2006.

Stephen Gandel   "A Divorced Dad Faces Fiscal Reality," *Money*, November 2005.

Marilyn Gardner   "Divorce's Shadow: When Older Parents Need Help," *Christian Science Monitor*, April 12, 2006.

Paul M. de Graaf and Matthijs Kalmijn   "Divorce Motives in a Period of Rising Divorce," *Journal of Family Issues*, April 2006.

Geoffrey Gray   "With This Ring (and This Contract), I Thee Wed," *New York*, March 27, 2006.

Julie Hanus   "Long-Term Love," *Utne*, March/April 2006.

Catherine T. Kenneyand and Sara S. McLanahan   "Why Are Cohabiting Relationships More Violent than Marriages?" *Demography*, February 2006.

Tamar Lewin   "Poll Says Even Quiet Divorces Affect Children's Paths," *New York Times*, November 5, 2005.

Maclean's   "The Don't-Ask, Don't-Tell Divorce," January 16, 2006.

Elizabeth Marquardt   "Fractured Family," *Christian Century*, February 7, 2006.

Julia McKinnell   "Yes, It's Wonderful. He's Left Me," *Maclean's*, January 23, 2006.

John Milton   "The Doctrine and Discipline of Divorce," *Wall Street Journal*, February 11, 2006.

National Catholic Reporter   "How the 'Good Divorce' Affects Children," March 24, 2006.

Marcia Pappas   "Divorce New York Style," *New York Times*, February 19, 2006.

People   "Bitter Battle," February 13, 2006.

Hilary Shenfeld   "A Smooth Divorce," *Newsweek*, September 5, 2005.

Susan Straight   "We Are (Still) Family," *New York Times Magazine*, December 18, 2005.

Peg Tyre   "The Secret Pain of Divorce," *Newsweek*, October 24, 2005.

USA Today magazine   "Splitting Up Drops Wealth by 77%," April 2006.

Hollida Wakefield   "Sexual Abuse Allegations in Custody Disputes," *Issues in Child Abuse Accusations*, Winter 2006.

Judith S.
Wallerstein

"Growing Up in the Divorced Family," *Clinical Social Work Journal*, Winter 2005.

Jay L. Zagorsky   "Marriage and Divorce's Impact on Wealth," *Journal of Sociology*, December 2005.

Jeffrey Zaslow   "Email Can Make Divorce Worse," *Wall Street Journal*, December 15, 2005.

Index